MONROE COLLEGE LIBRARY

D0085393

6358 4

Bleep!
Censoring Rock
and Rap Music

Recent Titles in
Contributions to the Study of Popular Culture

American Dark Comedy: Beyond Satire
Wes D. Gehring

Lois Weber: The Director Who Lost Her Way in History
Anthony Slide

Perry Mason: The Authorship and Reproduction of a Popular Hero
J. Dennis Bounds

A Call to Action: The Films of Ousmane Sembene
Sheila Petty, editor

Poet of Civic Courage: The Films of Francesco Rosi
Carlo Testa, editor

The Use of Arthurian Legend in Hollywood Film: From Connecticut Yankees to Fisher Kings
Rebecca A. Umland and Samuel J. Umland

Agent of Challenge and Defiance: The Films of Ken Loach
George McKnight, editor

Edison's Kinetoscope and Its Films: A History to 1896
Ray Phillips

The Last Modernist: The Films of Theo Angelopolous
Andrew Horton, editor

Theory and Practice of Classic Detective Fiction
Jerome H. Delamater and Ruth Prigozy, editors

The Detective in American Fiction, Film, and Television
Jerome H. Delamater and Ruth Prigozy, editors

Imagining the Worst: Stephen King and the Representation of Women
Kathleen Margaret Lant and Theresa Thompson, editors

Bleep! Censoring Rock and Rap Music

Betty Houchin Winfield
and Sandra Davidson,
Editors

Contributions to the Study of Popular Culture, Number 68

GREENWOOD PRESS
Westport, Connecticut • London

(handwritten, left margin: ML 3534 .B632 1999)

Library of Congress Cataloging-in-Publication Data

Bleep! : censoring rock and rap music / Betty Houchin Winfield and Sandra Davidson, editors.
   p.   cm.—(Contributions to the study of popular culture, ISSN 0198–9871 ; no. 68)
   An outgrowth of a 1993 international conference on rock and rap music and the mass media, "On the Beat: Rock 'n' Rap, Mass Media and Society."
   Includes bibliographical references and index.
   ISBN 0–313–30705–9 (alk. paper)
   1. Rock music—Censorship—United States.   2. Rap (Music)—Censorship—United States.   3. Music and society—United States. I. Winfield, Betty Houchin, date.   II. Davidson, Sandra, date. III. Title: Censoring rock 'n' rap music.   IV. Title: Censoring rock and rap music.   V. Series.
   ML3534.B632   1999
   306.4'84—dc21   98–15302
                   M N

British Library Cataloguing in Publication Data is available.

Copyright © 1999 by Betty Houchin Winfield and Sandra Davidson

All rights reserved. No portion of this book may be reproduced, by any process or technique, without the express written consent of the publisher.

Library of Congress Catalog Card Number: 98–15302
ISBN: 0–313–30705–9
ISSN: 0198–9871

First published in 1999

Greenwood Press, 88 Post Road West, Westport, CT 06881
An imprint of Greenwood Publishing Group, Inc.
www.greenwood.com

Printed in the United States of America

The paper used in this book complies with the Permanent Paper Standard issued by the National Information Standards Organization (Z39.48–1984).

10 9 8 7 6 5 4 3 2 1

Copyright Acknowledgments

The editors and publisher gratefully acknowledge permission for use of the following material:

"All the Things You Are." Written by Jerome Kern and Oscar Hammerstein II. Copyright © 1939 PolyGram International Publishing, Inc. Copyright Renewed. Used by Permission. All Rights Reserved.

"Sixty Minute Man"—William Ward, Rose Marks. © 1951—Fort Knox Music Inc. and Trio Music Co., Inc. Copyright renewed. Used by permission. All rights reserved.

"Sixty Minute Man." By: William Ward and Rose Marks. © 1951 (Renewed) Trio Music Co., Inc., Fort Knox Music, Inc. All Rights Reserved. Used by Permission.

Contents

"Let Me Count the Ways": Censoring Rock 'n' Rap Music

Betty Houchin Winfield

Bleep! Censoring Rock and Rap Music is about societal attempts to control rock 'n' rap music in a democracy. This book explains how governmental statutes, agency regulations, business controls and parents have tried to censor the music and when they have succeeded or why not. In particular, *Bleep!* discusses rock 'n' roll music, the offending lyrics and the surrounding youth culture beginning in the mid-1950s, and the rap beat, lyrics and hip-hop culture beginning in the mid-1980s. The book also focuses on the dilemma of a people who ideally believe in free expression as part of a democracy, yet at the same time are not absolute in that belief for various reasons. The limits of such tolerance about popular music are explained in *Bleep!*

The exploration of various aspects of rock and rap music censorship involves diverse and wide-ranging topics. The controls concern general societal reactions to new and alien music, racism, governmental responses, media outlets such as *Rolling Stone*, the *New York Times* and "The Ed Sullivan Show," and the music industry itself. All serve as gatekeepers, in a way controllers of the music and lyrics. The methodologies used here are qualitative: historical, legal and cultural. The chapter emphases go from general to specific.

In Chapter 1, "From Fine Romance to Good Rockin'—and Beyond: Look What They've Done to My Song," musicologist Michael J. Budds explains why American post–World War II popular music became so controversial in the 1950s, with examples and references to human sexuality and societal racism.

In Chapter 2, "Because of the Children: Decades of Attempted Controls of Rock 'n' Rap Music," press-government scholar Betty Houchin Winfield discusses the attempted prohibitions by American parents who organized and pressured government and industry toward controlling youth-based music and the subsequent youth culture. She traces how mostly Caucasian adults have censored under the guise of protecting children during the last 50 years. The overt fear is that children might emulate the behavior as emerging adults in new and shocking musical forms, lyrics and surrounding culture associated with rock and roll and rap music.

In Chapter 3, "Two Perspectives on Ice-T: 'Can't Touch Me': Musical Messages and Incitement Law," legal scholar Sandra Davidson examines the specific reasons why inciting musical messages of murder and killing cannot easily be censored with governmental statutes. She shows how the overall recent censorship attempts have been based on the music industry's internal economic pressure, in particular toward gangsta rappers, rather than as an enforcement of incitement law. She traces how difficult it is to enforce the incitement statutes concerning such extreme music messages.

In Chapter 4, "The Politics of Aesthetic Response: Cultural Conservatism, the NEA, and Ice-T," communication scholar David Slayden takes the Ice-T controversy one step further with a comparison to the National Endowment for the Arts (NEA) politics. He puts artistic expression within the context of aberrant art in American society by paralleling how the NEA's refusal to fund "objectionable" art coincides with the national attempts to censor rock lyrics, such as those of the song "Cop Killer." At the end of his chapter is an appendix on the NEA controls through guideline references to obscenity and the rejection process.

In Chapter 5, "Stern Stuff: Here Comes the FCC," Sandra Davidson applies some of David Slayden's similar appendices by demonstrating how the Federal Communications Commission (FCC) polices the broadcast airwaves through public pressure over indecency. She uses as an example how the FCC has consistently fined Howard Stern and the Infinity Broadcasting Corporation, by citing the protection of children as justification. Following her chapter are appendices on the FCC procedure for handing out fines and the related statutes on indecency.

In Chapter 6, "Music Lyrics: As Censored as They Wanna Be," legal scholar Jeffrey L. L. Stein traces how obscenity statutes have tried to censor rock lyrics from the early 1970s through the 2-Live Crew case and the Obscenity Decency Section with the 1996 Revised Federal Communication Act. Following this chapter is an appendix on the legal framework of obscenity and the related statutes.

In Chapter 7, "'Let's Spend the Night Together,' Uhhh, 'Some Time Together,' Making Rock Acceptable: 'The Ed Sullivan Show,'" Professor Stephen H. Wheeler takes a micro look at one particular instance of industry control of those lyrics. Wheeler shows how the tastes of popular television host Ed Sullivan controlled the television musical message during the 1950s and 1960s. Ed Sullivan insisted on compromises of the music lyrics and artists' behavior before rock musicians were allowed to perform on his show. The censorship was internal and initially it worked.

In Chapter 8, "*Rolling Stone*'s Response to Attempted Censorship of Rock 'n' Roll," Lindsey R. Fore traces the various controls over lyrics and associated culture in one media unit's response, *Rolling Stone* magazine. Fore shows how it was the mid-1980s before the magazine reacted to congressional hearings, proposed record labeling and the various justifications for censorship.

In Chapter 9, "Deconstructing the Hip-Hop Hype: A Critical Analysis of the *New York Times*' Coverage of African-American Youth Culture," American Culture Ph.D.

student Patrick B. Hill points out how another media institution internally censored and why. The *New York Times* acted as a cultural gatekeeper for new musical forms created by African-Americans. Hill compares how the news media framed the spot-news coverage of jazz and rap music, and the critical response by its own reporters, as negative. Hill refers to a study of news coverage concerning the emerging jazz in the 1920s, when it was becoming popular with society as a whole, and with the emerging rap and hip-hop culture in the 1980s, just as rap was becoming popular with middle-class white youths. In both instances, the music was portrayed as a conflict story.

Sandra Davidson compiled the appendices of statutes and legal cases following chapters four, five, and six.

"Bleeping" has long been a part of the diverse American society. As nineteenth-century French observer Alexis de Tocqueville once noted, intolerance runs alongside of a democracy. This book will more fully explain how and why.

Bleep! is an outgrowth of the University of Missouri 1993 conference, "On the Beat: Rock 'n' Rap, Mass Media & Society." The Missouri School of Journalism awarded seed money so scholars, students, performers, journalists, and rock and rap lovers could gather at the conference to learn from each other through popular music. The Office of the Provost, "The Blue Note" and the Freedom Forum for the First Amendment offered financial support to the conference. Censorship was an overriding theme. Although space does not allow a thank you to each of the faculty, friends and the many students who worked months on the conference, some special individuals worked particularly hard to make that fun-filled February week happen: R. Dean Mills, Lillian Dunlap, Richard King and Birgit Wassmuth. And, because of the support of the University of Missouri Research & Development Fund, Kathy Sharp's technical assistance and Janice Hume's and Cathy Jackson's library double-checking of references, this book project was completed. Thanks to them and to many others we can better understand our popular culture and the tolerance and intolerance of new musical forms.

From Fine Romance to Good Rockin'—and Beyond: Look What They've Done to My Song

Michael J. Budds

> You want to know what I think of that abomination, rock 'n' roll? I think it is a disgrace. Poison put to sound! When I hear it I feel very sad not only for music but for the people who are addicted to it. I am also very sorry for America—that such a great country should have nothing better to pour into the expectant ear of mankind than this raucous distillation of the ugliness of our times, performed by juveniles for juveniles. It is a terrible and sardonic trick of fate that the children of the present century should have to grow up with their bodies under continual bombardment from atomic fall-out and their souls exposed to rock 'n' roll.[1]
>
> —Pablo Casals, 1961

> Rock and roll fans, if even a portion of what the critics have said was true, by now would be stone deaf, with their minds burnt out by drugs, and their bodies wasted by excessive fornication. That none of this is true has never bothered rock opponents nor caused them to pause in their attacks. Rock-bashing has remained constant since the mid-1950s both in content and style.[2]
>
> —Linda Martin and Kerry Segrave, 1993

No musical repertory in Western civilization has aroused more controversy than rock and roll. No musical repertory has attracted so many powerful and self-righteous opponents. No musicians, viewed as a representative group, have taken such self-indulgent and often self-destructive delight in combining the roles of entertainer/artist and social outlaw. One need only invoke characterizations of three identifiable strains of this music—"shock rock," "cock rock," and "schlock rock"—to appreciate its power to send self-proclaimed protectors of American culture into fits of anguish. The implications of this music's underprivileged birthright, the complex temper of American society since its emergence as a mainstream phenomenon in the wake of World War II, its identification with the thought and behavior of teenagers, and its potential as a means for acquiring almost limitless wealth have all contributed to its perceived menace.

As a result, rock and roll has become a prime target for censorship campaigns by a host of special interest lobbies—religious, political, economic, and musical.[3] Such opposition, be it well-intentioned or vested in self-interest, has existed as an almost chronic condition throughout the music's rather short history. It can be argued, however, that the passion and energy expended in attempts to alter or suppress rock and roll expression have only spurred rockers to flaunt or exaggerate the "objectionable" aspects of their music and worldview in a spirit of defiant celebration. Rock fans have affirmed the behavior of musicians with unbridled enthusiasm and, by their adulation, have encouraged them to challenge the status quo.

At the heart of the issue is the mainstreaming of attitudes and practices, musical and otherwise, that represent fundamental departures from those institutionalized by the power culture since the colonization of the United States. This change in taste was even more dramatic—in fact, revolutionary—because it symbolized broad acceptance of the musical customs of black America and rural white America, sectors of society with little prestige and long dismissed as irrelevant to national standards and priorities. The actual musical language of rock and roll had long flourished, primarily in the South, without the sanction of upper- and middle-class white Americans who acknowledged the music of these outsiders begrudgingly as "race music" and "hillbilly music," respectively. What *was* new in the 1950s was an enthusiastic audience of middle-class teenagers from white America and a new designation "rock 'n' roll," which ironically is derived from blues imagery for sexual intercourse. These young people with their new fascination for minority music—with no malice aforethought, initially at least—proved to be an irrepressible force in reshaping many social patterns in American society during the second half of the twentieth century.

What made this transformation of American popular music the source of such violent debate is the very fact that it was generated and sustained by the youth of the power culture without the blessing of their parents. Few other musical movements have been defined so emphatically in terms of age. A house divided by rejection of parental preferences and the attending perception of betrayal and even subversion set the stage for a power struggle that marked the early years of rock and roll. Once the music established itself as more than an irritating fad and then quickly achieved status as the social emblem of rebellious youth, initial skirmishes faded as opponents regrouped to wage what has proved to be an ongoing war, one in which calls for censorship were raised as periodic battle cries and attempts at control took various forms.

Much of the negative response to rock and roll by voices in the establishment must be identified as both racist and elitist.[4] The music was roundly condemned by individuals who, with little experience and little understanding of its nature or history, judged it on the basis of what it was not and whose it was. The foreground importance assigned to the sounds of guitars and drums—often raucous, insistent, and amplified to penetrating levels of volume—was in itself perceived as an unabidable physical assault by detractors. In 1956, *Time* magazine, the prominent current events periodical of record for American society, helped set the tone for the national debate in its first report on rock and roll by describing the music in such loaded terms as "jungle," "juvenile delinquency," and "Hitler mass meetings."[5] Rock and roll, moreover, began its life as a symbol of integration, as an interracial music—with the participation of performers and consumers of both races. Although opportunities for African-American musicians were still systematically restricted, this circumstance alone was enough to rally the champions of entrenched segregation and bigotry.

In addition to the perceived threat to the society at large, the threat to the standing popular music industry was undeniable. Entertainment music in America was a highly lucrative business that directly affected the livelihood of countless individuals. Rather suddenly, the musical products of young Southern upstarts flooded the marketplace with stunning success. Serious loss of income and loss of control forced industry executives to adopt a defensive posture. Leaders of the recording industry went so far as to condemn the music of their competitors as socially irresponsible and morally corrupting. The editors of *Billboard* and *Variety*, trade magazines of the profession, called for self-policing and raised the specter of government censorship as the ultimate solution to the dilemma.[6] In a short time, of course, the industry—chastened by reality, bent on surviving, and enticed by obvious financial rewards—embraced the world of rock and roll by buying it up piece by piece. This transaction helped legitimize the music's hold on the American middle class, but it also introduced musical compromises dictated by purely commercial concerns and a sensational approach to merchandising. It also meant that, in the view of many, by the end of the 1950s the industry itself had become part of the problem.

In retrospect, it seems possible to identify a number of factors that help explain this radical change in musical taste. First of all, the popular song tradition of Tin Pan Alley, which had been centered in New York City and had flourished for more than three generations, began to show signs of wear. The search for fresh and compelling expression within the rather well-defined style became increasingly difficult. The traumatic events of World War II, moreover, made the sanitized worldview delivered in the snappy dance songs and dreamy love ballads that were hallmarks of the genre seem inappropriate or irrelevant to the new generation of youngsters. At the same time that Tin Pan Alley was reaching its peak in the songs of Gershwin, Kern, Rodgers, and Porter, two minority song traditions that had evolved from longstanding folk practice—the urban blues of black America and the country and western songs of rural white Southerners—entered the popular arena and reached a larger audience thanks to a process of commercialization that included recordings, radio stations, and more venues for live performance. The inexpensive portable transistor radio, a by-product of wartime technology, enabled young people to acquaint themselves with rhythm and blues as well as country and western music without parental knowledge or supervision.

The appeal of these new options can be directly related to perceived virtues not to be found in the typical Tin Pan Alley product: an obvious spontaneity and informality in terms of musical process, an emphatic approach to rhythm that satisfied the important desire to dance, an intense and sometimes extravagant display of emotion, and the unapologetic treatment of subjects considered taboo as well as traditional subjects treated in a more realistic manner. The latter aspect became a special focus for guardians of public morals because of the sexual content of many songs, couched in blunt everyday speech or in suggestive double entendres inherited from the blues. The much bally-hooed breakdown in reticence about sexual matters during the early years was, of course, but a prelude to the free speech aesthetic that came to characterize the rock and roll repertory as the decades passed.

The most conspicuous target for the would-be censor has always been the lyrics of rock and roll songs, which have been labeled from the very beginning as trivial, sexually suggestive, or even obscene. The difference in the nature of song texts, however, must be related to the traditions from which they spring. Song texts of mainstream America had long been influenced by the high culture of Europe, however watered down for middle-class consumption. Romantic love, the subject of the vast majority of all songs, was treated in a highly idealistic, typically sentimental manner. Although rarely profound, the language tended toward the poetic, preferring a high-priced vocabulary filled with euphemism and fully respectful of an unwritten, but widely sanctioned code of public propriety. Songs with texts overstepping this sensibility were banned by radio stations or deleted from the musical scores of Broadway and Hollywood.[7] Early in the nineteenth century, for example, Stephen Foster's Jeanie was "borne like a vapor on the summer air." In time, the popular song industry was infused with a generous helping of what has been identified as the Jewish-American immigrant's dream, the point of view of so many of its creators. Although the genteel character of song texts was updated to fit the times, the general approach remained unchanged.

Considering the lyrics of two well-known and fairly representative songs provides convincing evidence of the existence of strikingly different attitudes toward popular song in twentieth-century American society. The words of Jerome Kern's evergreen classic "All the Things You Are" (1939), written by Oscar Hammerstein II, stand as a model of Tin Pan Alley restraint and "prettification":

> You are the promised kiss of springtime
> That makes the lonely winter seem long.
> You are the breathless hush of evening
> That trembles on the brink of a lovely song.
> You are the angel glow that lights a star,
> The dearest things I know are what you are.
> Some day my happy arms will hold you,

And some day I'll know that moment divine
When all the things you are, are mine.

Such lyrics were valued for their sophistication, their cleverness, their calculated substance. They clearly address sexual issues—in this instance a yearning for a consummated love relationship—but unfold in a perfectly indirect manner, without any trace of vulgarity. The world they represent, it might be noted, is not necessarily the world as it ever was or is, but a world conceived in a delightful or bittersweet fantasy. After all, Tin Pan Alley songs were frequently generated for the escapist entertainment of the Broadway stage or the Hollywood film.

In terms of text, the song traditions of the African-American community and the rural white community reflected a level of realism and honesty that flew in face of the mainstream's rules of decorum and its penchant for romantic "sweetness." Not only were such songs cast in the unvarnished language of colloquial speech, they were often based on the life experience of the music's creators. In comparison to the Tin Pan Alley product, the earthy text of "Sixty-Minute Man" (1951), a rhythm and blues cross-over hit created by William Ward and Rose Marks and popularized by the Dominoes in the early 1950s, leaves little to the imagination.

Looka here, girls, I'm telling you now they call me lovin' Dan.
I rock 'em, roll 'em all night long: I'm a sixty-minute man.
If you don't believe I'm all I say, come up here and take my hand.
When I let you go, you'll cry, "Oh, yes, he's a sixty-minute man."
There'll be fifteen minutes of kissin', then you'll holler, "Please, don't stop."
There'll be fifteen minutes of teasin' and fifteen minutes of pleasin',
And fifteen minutes of blowin' my top.
If your man ain't treatin' you right, come up here and see old Dan.
I rock 'em, roll 'em all night long: I'm a sixty-minute man.

The words of this song are overtly sexual. They testify to an easy-going pride in the manly art of seduction with an explicitness judged as disarming and risqué in some quarters but normal and refreshing in others. One might easily argue that, in substance, the themes of these two songs share pronounced similarities. Yet in manner, they must be perceived and, in fact, were perceived as worlds apart. It is a matter of historical record that a majority of young people in the United States indicated their preference for the more realistic approach by their grand-scale enthusiasm for rock and roll during the second half of the twentieth century.

What has been impossible for the critics to accept or appreciate, I suspect, is that the institutionalization of rock and roll by young Americans effected a rather dramatic change in the function of popular music in the greater society after the mid-twentieth-century. It can be argued that, in general, Western societies have embraced popular music for its ability to entertain across age groups, typically in the spirit of light-hearted diversion and good humor. Even plaintive love songs contributed to a corporate "feel good" sensibility concerning the universal anguish of lost or doomed romance. When political topics were addressed, social conditions mitigated dissent as eccentric; any perception of insensitivity among those who lacked power was ignored. For members of the mainstream culture, this music was tuneful and often animated; it could typically be described as "pretty" or "nice"; the tone of the text was rarely confrontational or provocative.

The birthright of rock and roll, in contrast, demanded that this traditional function be redefined as American youth "fell into" power and began to exert influence on society, largely because of their number and their middle-class purchasing privileges. For, in addition to its entertainment value, rock and roll also must be judged as political and social to an unprecedented degree. Its point of view was conditioned initially by adolescent frustration and soon after by youthful cynicism, on the one hand, and idealism, on the other. This redefinition of popular song included forays into subjects and moods foreign to the mainstream's entertainment experience. Thanks mainly to the champions of the folk revival of the 1960s and the dynamic African-American musicians leading the Civil Rights Movement, serious—and highly volatile—problems such as social injustice, hypocrisy, war-mongering, and the destruction of the environment entered the rock and roll sensibility. Just as great a departure from custom was the introduction of song texts openly dealing with the darker sides of human nature. Such themes had been grist for various forms of fine art (literature, music, painting) since the earliest days of the century and certainly had found expression in the blues and folk song since their beginnings, but such grim preoccupations had never before entered the realm of the mainstream's commercial song until the Counterculture forced the issue during the 1960s. (A similar phenomenon must be observed in the subjects and nature of films directed to the American public during the same period.) The threat was undeniable and uncomfortable to many adults; the fact that teenagers were making it was radical, a cause for much handwringing by those threatened.

In a very real sense, then, rock and roll culture has come to accept a premise already in force in folk music and fine-art music, that the subject of music is the entire range of human experience. Whereas many advocates welcomed this openness in the spirit of uncensored expression and as evidence of the music's "coming of age," opponents redoubled their efforts and publicized their genuine horror, all the while repeating their time-honored battle cry that the personal and public behavior of young Americans is influenced directly and in the most negative way by experiencing this repertory of song. Much criticism, ranging from thoughtful to hysterical, has been focused on a cult of violence initially associated with the 1970s subcategories of punk and heavy metal and more recently with gangsta rap[8] and the "hate" rock of white supremacist groups. For decades, feminists have been especially outspoken in condemning misogynist words, images, and actions that have found a home in the male-dominated world of rock and roll.[9] It is, of course, impossible to defend a music that serves as an intentional vehicle of evil and hatred, but it also seems reasonable to believe that popular music can reflect as a faithful mirror not only the flaws of human nature but also socially constructed racism, fascism, sexism, anti-Semitism, elitism, and other plagues at work in contemporary culture.

In spite of the big-business packaging, there is, probably, no better record of what has concerned American teenagers in the second half of the twentieth century than rock and roll. From its commercial beginnings, it remains a music with an attitude, purposefully at odds with authority figures and social prescriptions. And, just as important, these concerns have often been communicated, without apology or embarrassment, in the common language of teenagers intent on carving out a meaningful identity for themselves and their peers. Although still shocking in some quarters, moreover, the casual use of profanities, the graphic references to sexual behaviors and drug use, and the open attacks on other cultural "sacred cows" have not been exclusive to rock and roll.

Because of its essential commercial application in American popular culture as dance-related song (the demand for new product) and because of the need of each new generation of American youth to identify itself musically according to its own terms, the history of rock and roll has unfolded in an often confusing succession of substyles or subgenres that represent a broad range of expression. Although it is useful to appreciate such diversity under the umbrella of rock-related popular music, such subcategories have always represented meaningful distinctions to connoisseurs, and, in fact, a number of them can be described rather discretely in musical and sociological terms. It is important to understand whether a particular "movement" uses the urban blues, the Anglo-American ballad, or the mainstream popular song as its point of departure. Was the music, for example, created by ambitious young Southerners with a first-hand knowledge of minority music, by middle-class African-American talents from Detroit groomed for entertainment glory, by turned-on and tuned-in Bohemians in San Francisco with a Counterculture agenda, or by the rappers of America's inner-cities caught "between the outlaw culture of the streets and the hardcore taste of the music business"?[10] It is, likewise, instructive to construct a profile of representative groups of musicians and to place their accomplishments in context.

The contributions of African-American musicians have always represented a vital force in this music's history. From the time of slavery, musical expression has served an especially significant purpose in black America as a means of communicating, preserving, and renewing a cultural identity under miserable social conditions. It is surely no coincidence that the most far-reaching influences of African-American music-making—in the form of rock and roll—occurred in American society at the same time that the greatest strides were being made in the energizing struggle for civil rights. African-American musicians such as Chuck Berry, Little Richard, Fats Domino, and Bo Diddley defined the early rock and roll style of the 1950s, just as their successors carried their community's musical banner forward to create soul of the 1960s, funk of the 1970s, and hip-hop of the 1980s. The power of such music attracted many white listeners as well. It also provided compelling models for both exploitation and genuine imitation by legions of white musicians. The careers of Elvis

Presley, Janis Joplin, and the Rolling Stones, to cite a few of the most obvious, would be unthinkable without the examples of African-American musicians.

As the twentieth century reaches its end, the circumstances surrounding rock and roll are more complicated than ever and as controversial as ever. The tradition appears more fragmented than before because of the preservation of historical styles alongside interest in newer ones and because of the participation of various constituencies of performers and listeners representing various ages and life-styles. There is one aspect of the tradition, however, that remains unchanged: the music created by young Americans for young Americans continues to alarm, shock, and challenge the social code; its opponents are just as prepared as ever to voice their own outrage, to wage their holy war, and to fight for censorship.

NOTES

1. Pablo Casals, "A Disgrace to Music," *Music Journal* XIX:1 (Jan. 1961), 18. The Spanish-born Casals (1876–1973) enjoyed an international career as a violoncello virtuoso and conductor and was revered as one of the finest musicians of his time. His harsh assessment of rock and roll must be understood as the perception of one whose life was devoted to European fine-art music.

2. Linda Martin & Kerry Segrave, *Anti-Rock: The Opposition to Rock 'n' Roll* (Hamden, CT: Archon Books, 1988; reprinted New York: Da Capo Press, 1993), vii. Although some commentators are willing to attribute the sordid lifestyles of various rock musicians as well as the deaths of several others to the music itself, it seems clear that many other factors must be considered.

3. The most comprehensive and systematic study of this phenomenon is probably Martin & Segrave's *Anti-Rock: The Opposition to Rock 'n' Roll*, as cited above. Another significant study addressing this issue in British society is Martin Cloonan, *Banned! Censorship of Popular Music in Britain, 1967–1992* (Aldershot, Hampshire: Arena, 1996); see especially Chapter 2, "Censorship: Some Characteristics of the Debate."

4. "Elitist" is used here to designate an attitude of perceived superiority or privilege.

5. "Yeh-Heh-Heh-Hes, Baby," *Time* LXVII:25 (18 June 1956), 54.

6. See the editorials "Control the Dim-Wits," *Billboard* LXVI (25 Sept. 1954); and Abel [Green], "A Warning to the Music Business," *Variety* CXCVII:12 (23 Feb. 1955), 2.

7. The grand exception appears to be songwriter/composer Cole Porter (1891–1964), whose witty but suggestive lyrics earned for him the nickname "the genteel pornographer" from Cecil Smith in *Musical Comedy in America* (New York: Theatre Arts Books, 1950).

8. See, for example, Ronin Ro, *Gangsta: Merchandising the Rhymes of Violence* (New York: St. Martin's Press, 1996).

9. An early example is Marion Meade, "Does Rock Degrade Women?," *New York Times* II (14 March 1971) , 13, 22.

10. Martha Bayles, *Hole in Our Soul: The Loss of Beauty & Meaning in American Popular Music* (New York: The Free Press, 1994; reprinted Chicago: University of Chicago Press, 1996), 355.

2

Because of the Children: Decades of Attempted Controls of Rock 'n' Rap Music

Betty Houchin Winfield

> For people in the entertainment industry in this country, we applaud your creativity and your worldwide success, and we support your freedom of expression. But you do have a responsibility to assess the impact of your work and to understand the damage that comes from the incessant, repetitive mindless violence and irresponsible conduct that permeates our media all the time.
>
> —Bill Clinton, State of the Union Address
> January 24, 1995

Bill Clinton, a "boomer" of early rock 'n' roll who adopted as a campaign song the rock classic "Don't Stop Thinking About Tomorrow," points out a popular cultural censorship dilemma between free expression and social responsibility. Creativity by its very nature is different; by being new and appealing, music also can be monetarily successful. Yet, as a form of free expression, the music through its sounds and lyrics can urge deviant, suggestive, even violent behavior of those the most impressionable —the young—and thus impact the community. Such possible effects alarm many adults, including the president. And, to protect the children, censorship in a free society can be justified. This chapter discusses the American dilemma of free musical expression, particularly the rock and rap music of the past 45 years, and social controls and censorship.

In the larger picture of a democratic society, an ideal community without defined classes, culture would be diverse. In this model, no specific group defines the culture's music. Creativity would reign in a marketplace of music. No rules would limit the musical expression; anything would be possible. As one of the oldest forms of human expression, music freely appeals not only to any age, but also to an individual's gambit of emotions and intellect.

During the latter half of this century, the reaction to rock 'n' roll and rap music has become a clash of cultures. There is no consensus regarding musical tastes. In many ways, biases play a large role in the reaction. Because creativity goes back to the roots of a culture, the clashes occur between the roots of European and African musical sounds and words. In Euro-centric music, creativity means change, sometimes quite subtle, with one melodic message building upon and replacing another. The melody is central. Composers try new musical forms and methods, new sounds. Different lyrics often interact, building upon a western melodic sequence of sounds. Creativity in Afro-centric music depends on repetition and the revitalizing sounds of the beat. The rhythm is primary. The words fit the beat and overtly express human emotions. Such constants are all the more noticeable in rock and rap music that is predominately tied to African sounds and explicit lyrics.

Despite court rulings that such music and other cultural expressions are protected under the First Amendment,[1] the reality is that many American adults, particularly Caucasian adults, have historically disliked non-European sounds, especially when they first heard them. Historically, the Afro-rhythmic sounds were alien and the words are shockingly suggestive to Euro-centric ears. In the historical progression of the blues-jazz-rock-rap songs, critics, especially those of European heritage, accused such music and their composers of causing disruptions to cultural values, of inciting violence and of being detrimental to society.

At the same time, teenagers sought not just new musical sounds but voices and words to speak to them individually as they forged adult identities. The music was ever-appealing. Adolescent upheavals also meant surviving stresses about sexuality, romance, morality, parents, authority and government. The emerging new forms of rock and rap music can speak personally to these older children.

Because teens' tastes are still forming, still impressible, as many approach adulthood their quest centers around the music, if not in lyrics and sounds, then culturally by breaking previous modes with taboo words and musical actions. The biggest taboos concern incitement to violence toward women and authority figures such as the police and the word "fuck" and other sexually explicit utterances. With such music obviously aimed at teens, parents worried about possible out-of-control rebellion, and cultural and societal depravity. The fear was incitement, possibly leading minors to aberrant behavior, such as misogyny, racism and violence.

In fact, rock 'n' roll and rap music have become the blame for what was wrong with the country's emerging adults. Popular music that not only sounds different but has suggestive lyrics aimed at children frightens many parents. The response has been a series of attempted controls that have encompassed government as well as economic and commercial forms of censorship.

The justification for such controls is based on fears about the effects of rock and rap words and music: that such expressions might cause youth to become ungovernable, unlikely to follow society's rules. The possible effects include modeling of bizarre behavior, as well as imitating alien sounds, speaking taboo words, emulating violent lyrics, fulfilling sexual desires, copying the performers' outlandish antics and being overwhelmed by extreme audience reactions. Many adults see the musicians as instigators, whose compositions and actions violate society's norms and appear to encourage sexual antics and savagery such as murder, drug use and suicide. Because music can convey feelings and emotions, the danger of this music is clear and present to those who fear these behaviors, and fear it enough to justify censorship and control.

The clear-and-present-danger designation has historically meant that the state can regulate speech if the danger is too great and obvious. In other words, free expression in the United States would not be absolute.[2] However, those areas that have not warranted protection include pornography and obscenity which children can access. The Federal Communications Commission (FCC) legally regulates broadcasted speech of taboo words and prime time messages to a greater degree than any attempted controls over written expressions. Despite giving Constitutional protection to many forms of entertainment,[3] the Supreme Court never has decided what degree of free-expression protection could be afforded to music, outside of copyright protections.

Beyond legal controls, censoring music can be indirect. Consumers have been urged to boycott concerts and to refuse to purchase the music that parents and other adults have publicized as detrimental. Businesses and discount chain mega-stores respond to public pressures and refuse to carry the offending music, especially the music labeled obscene or violent. The industry can censor itself and chill expression, no matter how financially successful. The country's youth, as the prime consumers of new musical forms, have long purchased tapes, records and CDs, listened to radio, watched MTV and attended concerts.[4] Rock in its many forms into Rap topped the musical purchases by dollar value.[5] Industry executives, Time-Warner for one, avoid those artists or groups who are so controversial as to hurt sales. Besides being influenced to some degree by the youths' musical preferences, music companies do react to strong parental groups who protest that particular lyrics are too violent or too sexually suggestive and obscene. And some individuals have sued musicians and music businesses because of suspected effects to them and their families.

Public officials react to the controversial music with moral outrage and propose laws as a means of protecting the nation's children and the rest of society. Organized groups pressure appointed and elected officials to do something under the guise of protecting youth and the society in general. In recent years, former Secretary of Education William Bennett along with C. Delores Tucker and other governmental and parental leaders especially reacted to rap songs about urban violence. In the 1980s, after hearing such explicit lyrics urging masturbation in "Darling Nikki" on Prince's *Purple Rain* album and in some heavy metal songs, a group of politicians' wives, the Parents' Music Resource Center (PMRC), pushed for legislation for some type of labeling that would warn of obscenity and deviant behavior.[6] Warning labels on compact discs, tapes and printed lyrics have become standard parts of the product. However in many cases, those warning stickers only increased sales of almost-banned products. The leader in the movement to educate parents about inciting and suggestive movies and music, Tipper Gore, stated then that censorship was not her aim. Rather, Gore argued, additional speech would counteract the effects of such pornography.[7]

Attempts to apply long-term obscenity or indecency statutes to music have failed.

Those laws have historically been based on value judgments. Messages that offend one person may appeal to another; many times the expressions are generation-bound. In creative and artistic endeavors, music is evaluated individually as to song, album, and performer. For a message to be declared obscene it must meet all parts of a three-prong legal test, based on the 1973 *Miller* decision: "whether the average person, applying contemporary community standards would find the work, taken as a whole, appeals to the prurient interest," "whether the work depicts in a patently offensive way sexual conduct, specifically defined by applicable state law," and "whether the work has any redeeming social value."[8] The Supreme Court also said that a state could define obscenity for minors under the age of 17 and prohibit the sale of obscenity to them.[9] What is still emerging doctrine is how to apply these tests to music (see chapters 4, 5 and 6).

Even though it has been difficult to apply the *Miller* obscenity test because of the possible artistic or political value defense, attempts have been made. In the case of Luke Records and 2-Live Crew's popular 1992 album, *As Nasty as They Wanna Be*, the Eleventh Circuit Court of Appeals found that the obscenity test had been misapplied, and that the recording was not legally obscene because it did not meet the third legal prong concerning redeeming social value.[10]

The current constitutional debate over heavy metal rock and gangsta rap music is not just about the explicit language but also advocacy, an act of incitement to violence. Previous censorship concerns over incitement dealt with political speech. In 1925, Justice Holmes wrote in the *Gitlow v. New York* dissent, "every idea is an incitement. It offers itself for belief, and if believed, it is acted on unless some other belief outweighs it, or some failure of energy stifles the movement at birth."[11] Incitement in reference to rap music concerns brutality and physical injury. Although not covered by the *Miller* standard, this means that the state, even though it has broad interests in children's welfare, bears a heavy burden of justifying regulations. The illusive community's standards would not be used.

Historically, when music has flouted society's norms on behavior and sounds, various internal or external controls have been instituted or the music was changed in some way to make it more acceptable. Traditional blues singers, facing record and broadcast censorship to prevent public outrage, formulated new imagery to circumvent the record company censors. By the mid-1950s, rock 'n' roll, with its mass appeal to white youth during the early civil rights movement, was particularly suspect. Shocking to many adults was not just the startling sexual rock lyrics, but also the performers' suggestive stage manner, double entendre phrases, and guttural noises.[12] The "senseless and incoherent" sounds "deviated from the outward symbols of respectability," according to youth scholar James R. McDonald. In the late 1950s, when "Rock Around the Clock" became the teenage national anthem, many adults tried to link rock 'n' roll to teenage open sexuality and rebellion.[13]

Adult America denounced rock as the devil's music, full of messages about sex, drugs, perversion, communism, atheism, miscegenation, and criminal activities. "Such music is subversive and must be stopped," became the cry. Besides creating public outrage, the new rock music separated youth from their parents and threatened "normalcy." After *Brown v. Kansas* (1954) white youth appeared to be drawn to black performers such as Chuck Berry and Little Richard.[14]

With prevailing social racism, rock songs by African Americans, no matter how creative, were suspect and an affront to the openly segregationist views of the 1950s and 1960s. To be financially successful, black music became marginalized in the popular culture with white "covers." Many black musicians received little or no compensation when their songs were recorded by whites. Scholar Marilyn Flood points to the numerous early rock songs released in the rhythm-and-blues field that later became popular music hits when covered by white artists. For example, Pat Boone covered "Ain't that a Shame" by Fats Domino and "Tutti Fruitti" by Little Richard.[15] When rap music began appearing in the public consciousness by the mid-1980s, it represented a joining, gang-type of expression. The adult fear was that American youth would indeed "join" and empathize with the black adolescents' urban experience. Despite the fact that there were some white rappers, black artists dominated gangsta rap with black codes and street lingo explicit enough to be understood. Even though almost three-quarters of all rap albums were bought by white youth, rap music remained a black phenomenon. The lyrics confronted audiences with issues of racism, sexism, and black feelings toward white authority. Unlike adult concerns about heavy metal music's effects upon the fragile minds of a few troubled individuals, rap music was thought to cause a volatile reaction from entire audiences. In April 1989, Tone Loc's "Wild Thing" was accused of being the cause of the Central Park "wilding" rape. The suspicion was that black youth were unthinking, animal-like, and ready to erupt into a frenzy of "wilding" and rioting.

Adults, primarily white adults, had an overriding fear that black youth were dry kindling, ready to burst into flame with any stray spark. Inflammatory songs such as "Cop Killer" could incite an entire race to murder the nation's police. Unlike previous reactions to musical changes, such anxieties were aimed not at particular artists as individuals, but at an entire racial group.[16]

The accusations about rap lyrics became not just a racial issue, but also reflected gender and social issues concerning sexism, sexual harassment, rape, and murder. Much of rap has been sexually explicit, such as *As Nasty as They Wanna Be* by 2-Live Crew, which included the songs "Me So Horny" and "Dick Almighty." The reaction was outrage over Ice-T's "Cop Killer," from the album *Body Count*, which infuriated people with the lyrics "Die, die, die, pig, die!" Public outcry against "Cop Killer" included death threats against the record company employees until Ice-T announced he would pull "Cop Killer" from the album. Internationally, Irish radio stations and Australian live shows also banned "Cop Killer." [17]

The argument was that censorship was warranted; rap lyrics were of graphic nature with sadistic and masochistic material. Rap music resonated with a wide range of listeners and became a weekly staple on MTV. Political at many levels, boastful and angry, rap lyrics and sounds resonated with primitive beats that emphasized conflict. Rap upset the prevailing view that the lyrics do not matter. The charge was that groups, such as 2-Live Crew, had lustful lyrics that encouraged sexual exploits and incited violent confrontations. Yet, the Supreme Court has not been confronted with what musical lyrics were at stake.[18] In July 1990, 2-Live Crew's recording became the subject of the "Donahue" and "Geraldo" shows with musicians such as Frank Zappa and Axl Rose speaking on the right of musicians to express themselves musically, no matter what the response. Luther Campbell, the leader of 2-Live Crew, came out with a solo single, "Banned in the USA." Because of the free-expression principles involved, Bruce Springsteen granted Campbell permission to use the chorus from "Born in the USA."[19] Scholar Henry Gates argued in a letter to the *New York Times* that the case of 2-Live Crew "tells more about the American psyche" than about the group.[20] Yet, no matter which racial ethnicity, which artist or composer, extreme sexual or violent lyrics and antics have a long history of musical censorship. Censors argue that the possible appeal to the youth-emotions would be too great.

Banning suggestive words is not new, especially for written expression. Over 100 years ago, Anthony Comstock and his Society for the Suppression of Vice stifled all kinds of written expression, especially those words and pictures concerning sexuality. In nineteenth century Italy, Verdi's operas, such as "La Traviata," were considered so controversial that the composer wrote different librettos to fit different locales. Community standards ruled even then.

For over 50 years on radio, certain songs' sexual lyrics were unacceptable. NBC banned 147 recorded songs in 1940; songs such as "Love for Sale" could only be broadcast as an instrumental.[21] By the late 1950s, Congress held hearings on rock music, ostensibly on the possible conflicts of interest on the part of the business promoting rock 'n' roll to broadcast stations. The actual reason may have been to investigate the menace of uncontrolled youth and rock 'n' roll.[22]

When the Supreme Court upheld the FCC's authority to regulate indecent speech in 1978, the rock 'n' roll community could only expect some kind of broadcast censorship.[23] The "indecency" label meant nonconformity with accepted standards of morality, a national standard for judging indecency complaints. Initially, the FCC announced that indecent speech could only be broadcast between midnight and 6 AM. By 1988, President Ronald Reagan signed a bill to make the ban total, regardless of the hour. When challenged, the FCC argued that a total ban accomplished the government's compelling interest in protecting children.[24]

The political history had been clear. Under the guise of protecting the youth, in the early 1970s, Vice-President Spiro Agnew condemned the media for promoting drug addiction by broadcasting drug-oriented lyrics. The FCC responded in 1973 with a Public Notice, "In Re License Responsibility to Review Records Before They Broadcast," as a reminder to radio station licensees of their responsibility to serve the public interest and become familiar with lyric content. Broadcasters were to review all records before they were broadcast. While the Court of Appeals for the District of Columbia upheld the FCC notice and later the clarifying order, the court also ruled that the penalties were unreasonable. If a station did not understand obscene lyrics, then it could not be penalized. The FCC notice included 22 songs with drug-oriented lyrics, including the accused Peter, Paul and Mary's "Puff, the Magic Dragon" and the Beatles "I Get by with a Little Help from My Friends" and "Lucy in the Sky with Diamonds." These "do not play list" songs lost broadcast access and were in effect censored.[25]

During the 1960s and 1970s, many songs and well-known performers became part of the public debate over music censorship. For example, close watchers and listeners declared the popular "Louie, Louie" by Richard Berry, recorded by the Kingsmen in 1963, to be obscene. The FBI, after a two-and-a-half year pursuit with agents in six cities, finally decided, "We don't know what we're dealing with, and it seems to be gibberish, but that gibberish must be presumed guilty until all rampantly paranoid parents and teachers stop believing the fantasies of teenagers suffering from hormonal overload."[26] The FCC played "Louie, Louie" backward and forward at 78, 45, and 33 rpm in an attempt to discover what suggestive message the song gave. The FCC verdict was that "the song is unintelligible at any speed."[27]

Since the 1950s, attempts have been made by the entertainment industry to censor the songs or the performers. To sing live on Ed Sullivan's Show, the Rolling Stones promised to change "Let's Spend the Night Together" to "Let's Spend Some Time Together." They didn't. Because Paul McCartney's 1992 "Big Boys Bickering," an ecological song about the ozone and the bickering at the Rio Earth Summit, included the word "fuck" seven times, it was considered unsuitable for playing on MTV, even on MTV's special, "Paul McCartney Up Close." The shock value of saying "fuck" today should have subsided since controversy over the Dead Kennedys' 1981 "Too Drunk to Fuck."[28]

In one sense, prohibiting particular songs creates a type of "in-your-face" partnership between the artists and their audiences. When the German group Die Arzte was banned by their CBS label from releasing a song, "Helmut Kohl Beats His Wife," the group released the song itself to popular acclaim. When the musicians planned to perform and promote their album in Munich, "Helmut Kohl" had been left off, and the hall was surrounded by police. Police told the band that if they sang the song, they would be arrested. Die Arzte shared its dilemma with the audience, and while the musicians played the music, the audience sang the words for them. No one was arrested.[29]

Since the early 1970s, American government officials have been more outspoken in their opinions about the effects of various musical forms aimed at youth. The music paralleled the civil rights movement, the Vietnam War protests, the assassination of charismatic leaders, the "credibility gap," the "generation gap," the "gender gap," and environmental concerns. American youth were already politicized, and their ideology permeated the music.[30] President Richard Nixon tried to deport John Lennon in 1970 because of the political content of Lennon's musical lyrics and what Nixon called Lennon's deviant behavior. Vice-President Spiro Agnew charged that rock lyrics were "threatening to destroy our national strength." Performers were fined for their sexual, drug and anti-war messages. For example, Country Joe McDonald with his "Feel Like I'm Fixing to Die Rag" was fined $500 in Massachusetts as a "lewd, lascivious and wanton person in speech and behavior." The United States Senate, led by Senator James Buckley, investigated the "drugola" relationship between drugs and rock music. Buckley accused CBS and Columbia Records of using drugs to pay the disc jockeys in return for promoting particular songs and performers.[31] At the same time, the FBI made extensive reports on John Lennon (92 pages), Jim Morrison (91 pages), and Elvis Presley (87 pages).[32] Federal officials connected the music's political messages and the power of resistance from the mid-1960s into the early 1970s.

Such official responses continue as the Bill Clinton quote at the beginning of this chapter attests. The justification has continued to be to protect the youth. President Reagan proclaimed that the media were providing children with "the glorification of drugs and violence and perversity" of heavy metal. The PMRC successfully pushed for Senate hearings on volunteer labeling of lyrics and Jesse Jackson's PUSH advocated a rating system because of the effect of the "porn-rock" on inner-city youth. Despite arguments against labeling as "forced speech written by governments and imposed on the private parties," there was only mild resistance.[33] The record companies adopted a "warning sticker," "Parental Advisory: Explicit Lyrics," and a rating system. Seventeen states passed legislation that went one step further and targeted the sale of popular music to minors by including sound recordings in their states' existing "harmful to minors" statutes.

By the 1990s, companies, such as Wax Works, Trans World chains, Wal-Mart, and K-Mart, stopped carrying albums and singles labeled for explicit lyrics. Especially targeted were rap albums with violence and sexually explicit labels. The record industry (RIAA) agreed to print a warning label on the albums' back covers or to print the lyrics either on the back cover or on sheets planted under the plastic album cover. After the RIAA announced the standardized labeling system in April 1990, 13 states withdrew proposed laws.[34] Washington state's 1992 statute, similar to other states', was aimed at music "potentially 'harmful to minors.'" The statute was found unconstitutional on the free-speech grounds of prior restraint.[35]

Political figures such as Oliver North and Vice-President Dan Quayle made public statements supporting a police widow's suit against Tupac Shakur and the album *2pacalypse Now* for the rap song "Sister Souljah." The uproar over possible effects of incitement and advocacy had also concerned heavy metal artists, such as Ozzy Osbourne and Judas Priest, whose music was mostly aimed at blue-collar working-class whites. Priest, who appeared to urge satanic worship on his *Stained Class* album, was charged with causing a 1985 teen suicide attempt and the eventual deaths of two youth fans through subliminal messages.

The marketplace can censor the music too, albeit indirectly. In fact, music that lacks a potential market has faced insurmountable obstacles in the efforts to secure recording contracts, promotion sales, and air-play. Many times the reaction has been racial bias. At the same time that black music achieved mainstream status, much of the jazz, blues, and 1960s rhythm-and-blues lost racial identification and some of its meaning. Government censorship was based on content restrictions—the clear-and-present-danger and obscenity tests by the states—but the industry's self-restraint of the music was the result of the power of the marketplace. Billboard's chart-compilations historically determined the rankings of popular singles and albums. By the 1990s, with new computer technology adopted, black music performances on singles' charts improved dramatically.[36]

The record companies, many of whom began as mom-and-pop operations, went to a marketed consumer product by the 1980s.[37] The companies with booming subsidiary enterprises were captives of the PMRC demands. By the 1990s, music companies and music stores refused to sell rock and rap music labeled as violent and sexually explicit to anyone under 16. Many mainstream nonmusic retailers, such as Wal-Mart, subsequently refused to carry certain labels and undoctored album covers.

By selling stickered music only to those over 16 years of age, American youth have limited access to some music, especially heavy metal rock and rap.

Violence and extreme behavior as found in rap lyrics sells. Before he was murdered in Las Vegas in 1996, Tupac Shakur, one of gangsta rap's biggest stars, was encouraged to be extreme in his antics and rap lyrics by the multimillion-dollar record industry. His first album, *All Eyez on Me*, released in early 1996 for Death Row Records, sold over five million units. The more confrontational he was, the more newsworthy he was, and the more his releases sold. To some he became a hero; to others, a demon. According to Connie Bruck's *New Yorker* (1997) examination, Tupac was caught in the middle between his own character and the commercial image his record company required, and he paid the highest price of all.[38]

Public opinion has been insidiously chilling, too. After the rap group N.W.A., with "Straight Outta Compton," and Ice-T, with "Cop Killer," enraged police officers, many adults organized boycotts, not only of the albums, but also the concerts.[39] An incitement charge meant no free-speech protection if the danger seemed immediate and likely and if the intent was to stimulate an illegal action.[40] Although music is protected speech under the First Amendment and there is a right of public access to such speech, states and cities passed statutes banning rap or heavy metal concerts because of possible incitement. These laws may not fulfill the First Amendment requirement that such statutes be content-neutral, [41] but, the courts generally respect a city's interest "in attempting to preserve the quality of urban life." And unreasonably high insurance requirements for concerts have become another form of prior restraint.

Even though a municipality cannot deny rap or heavy metal performers access to a public forum,[42] the issue may be what form of access is allowed. When New York City cut off the power for Rock Against Racism (RAR) at a 1989 concert after repeatedly requesting that the group lower the volume, the audience became abrasive and disruptive. The courts agreed with the city's guidelines concerning excessive noise and the use of the Central Park Naumberg Acoustic Bandshell.[43]

Cities banned concerts because of the young audience and a perceived sexually charged, drug-ridden, and possibly violent atmosphere. And neighborhoods successfully complained about excessive noise as well as potential disorder.[44] For example, the Grateful Dead was forbidden to perform in many places because of potential illegal drug use and violation of community mores.

By the 1990s, visual displays were as important as music. MTV, founded in 1981, was revolutionary in that audiences could hear the lyrics, learn the code words, and see the artists up close without having to go to clubs or rock concerts. The distinction between advertising and entertainment disappeared with MTV as a trend-setter, promoting youth and youth culture. Aimed at America's 14–25-year-olds, MTV switched to rap before mainstream radio stations did. Adult pressure groups, such as the PMRC, began protesting not just the words, but the visual images of sex and violence filling such videos. Yet this youth network, while more explicit in visual content, refused to play music with sexually explicit words, such as "fuck."[45]

Presidential candidates in the 1990s openly went after extreme expression. Bill Clinton attacked Sister Souljah of Public Enemy for her outspoken 1992 remarks. In

1996, Bob Dole and Bill Clinton urged industry responsibility for their musical expression with internal censorship. These politicians' comments have been among the many adult attempts to control the rock and rap expressions by arguing the defense of children. The music may represent aesthetic and artistic freedom, but to such political leaders and many adults, the music also represents more than the musical sounds or the lyrics. The music embraces attitudes about urban life and how to respond to personal relationships and what to do, to social values and what to embrace. Such popular music aimed at youth has been, and will continue to be, political, with lyrics expressing attitudes about social mores, civil rights, racism, war participation, sexism, the environment, the urban blight, police brutality, and authority. Rock and rap music, representing the generational tension in western society, is a recurring conflict with attempts to censor, to "bleep" the message, the rock 'n' rap musical expression—because of the children.

NOTES

1. *Ward v. Rock Against Racism*, 109 S. Ct. 2753 (1989); *Citizens to Save WIFM v. Federal Communications Commission*, 506 F.2d 246, 251 (D.C. Cir. 1974). See *Cinevision Corp. v. City of Burbank*, 745 F.2d 560, 567 (9th Cir. 1984), cert. denied, 471 U.S. 1054 (1985) where the Court of Appeals for the 9th Circuit agreed that "music is a form of expression that is protected by the First Amendment."

2. *Schenck v. U.S.*, 249 U.S. 47 (1919).

3. *Schad v. Borough of Mount Ephraim*, 452 U.S. 61 (1981); *Southeastern Promotions, Ltd. v. City of Atlanta*, 334 F. Supp. 634 (N.D. Ga. 1971). See *Cinevision Corp. v. City of Burbank*, 745 F. 2d 560, 567 (9th Cir. 1984), cert. denied, 471 U.S. 1054 (1985).

4. In 1984, the Record Industry Association of America showed that children aged 10 to 14 accounted for nine percent of all purchases of rock records, children 15 to 19 accounted for 22 percent, and the remaining records were purchased by buyers over 20 years of age. See Cecile Berry and David Wolin, "Comment, Regulating Rock Lyrics: A New Wave of Censorship?" *Harvard Journal on Legislation* 23:2 (Summer 1986): 606, which cites the *Recording Industry Association of America, Inc., Inside the Recording Industry: A Statistical Overview* 12 (1985).

5. Steve Jones, *Rock Formation, Music, Technology, and Mass Communication: Foundations of Popular Culture*, Vol. 3 (Newbury Park, CA: Sage Publications, 1992), p. 2.

6. Anthony DeCurtis, "The Eighties," *Present Tense, Rock & Roll and Culture*, edited by Anthony DeCurtis (Durham, NC: Duke University Press, 1992), p. 6.

7. Tipper Gore, *Raising PG Kids in an X-Rated Society* (Nashville: Abingdon Press, 1987), p. 22.

8. *Miller v. California*, 413 U.S. 15 (1973).

9. *Ginsberg v. New York*, 390 U.S. 629, 638 (1968).

10. *Luke Records, Inc. v. Navarro*, 960 F.2d 134 (11th Cir. 1992).

11. *Gitlow v. People of State of New York*, 268 U.S. 652, 45 S.Ct. 625, 69 L.Ed. 1138 (1925).

12. Marilyn J. Flood, "Lyrics and the Law: Censorship of Rock-and-Roll in the United States and Great Britain," *New York Law School Journal of International and Comparative Law* 12:3 (Fall 1991), 402.

13. James R. McDonald, "Censoring Rock Lyrics: A Historical Analysis of the Debate,"

Youth and Society 19:3 (March 1988), 296.

14. Ibid.

15. Flood, "Lyrics and the Law," p. 401 at 23.

16. Jason Talerman, "The Death of Tupac: Will Gangsta Rap Kill the First Amendment?" *Boston College Third World Law Journal* 14:1 (Winter 1994), 138. Talerman quotes Chuck Phillips, "The Uncivil War: The Battle Between the Establishment and Supporters of Rap Music Opens Old Wounds of Race and Class," *Los Angeles Times Calendar*, 19 July 1992, 6.

17. Emily Campbell, "Obscenity, Music and the First Amendment: Was the 2-Live Crew Lively?" *Nova Law Review* 15:1 (Winter 1991), 159–240.

18. Ibid.

19. Ibid., pp. 165–166.

20. *New York Times*, 15 July 1990.

21. A. Dougherty, "From 'Race Music' to Heavy Metal: A Fiery History of Protests," *People Weekly* 25 (Sept. 16, 1985), 52; Edward J. Vatz, "You Can't Play That, A Selective Chronology of Banned Music: 1850–1991," *School Library Journal* 37:7 (July 1991), 16.

22. Trent Hill, "The Enemy Within: Censorship in Rock Music in the 1950s," *Present Tense, Rock & Roll and Culture*, edited by Anthony DeCurtis (Durham, NC: Duke University Press, 1992), pp. 59, 63, 65.

23. *FCC v. Pacifica Foundation*, 438 U.S. 726 (1978).

24. Marilyn Flood, "Lyrics and the Law," (1991), p. 413.

25. *Yale Broadcasting Co. v. FCC*, 478 F.2d, 594, 598 (D.C. Cir. Ct.) cert. denied, 414 U.S. 914 (1973).

26. Dave Marsh, *Louie Louie* (New York: Hyperion, 1993), pp. 117, 135.

27. T. Moran, "Sounds of Sex," *New Republic* (Aug. 12, 19, 1985), 14–16.

28. David Holden, "Pop Go the Censors," *Index on Censorship* 22 (May/June 1993), 11–12.

29. Ibid., 13.

30. James Lull, *Popular Music and Communication* 2nd ed. (Newbury Park, CA: Sage Publication, 1992), see in particular pp. 6–7.

31. B. Fong-Torres, "Drugola Inquiry: Senator Claims Columbia Gag," *Rolling Stone* (Aug. 16, 1973), 8.

32. McDonald, "Censoring Rock Lyrics," p. 301.

33. Marilyn Flood, "Lyrics and the Law," 417.

34. Ibid.

35. Jim McCormick, "Protecting Children from Music Lyrics: Sound Recordings and 'Harmful to Minors' Statutes," *Golden Gate University Law Review* 23:1–2 (Spring 1993), 689–692, 698–699.

36. Jim Sernoe, "The Performance of Black Music on *Billboard* Magazine's Pop Music Charts," paper presented to the Minorities and Communication Division, Association for Education in Journalism and Mass Communication conference, Atlanta, August 1994, p. 2.

37. See a full discussion on this in Fred Goodman's *The Mansion on the Hill: Dylan, Young, Geffen, Springsteen and the Head-on Collision of Rock and Commerce* (New York: Times Books/Random House), 1997.

38. Connie Bruck, "The Takedown of Tupac," *The New Yorker* (July 7, 1997), 46–65.

39. DeCurtis, *Present Tense*, p. 6.

40. *Brandenberg v. Ohio*, 395 U.S. 444 (1969).

41. *Schad v. Borough of Mount Ephriam*, 452 U.S. 61, 65 (1981), where the First Amendment protects live entertainment, including musical works. See *Young v. American Mini Theatres*, 427 U.S. 50, 77, rehearing denied, 429 U.S. 873 (1976); *Cinevision*, 745 F.2d at 574.

42. Jeanine Natter, "Un-Ban the Banned Band, A First Amendment Perspective on Banning Concerts," *Entertainment and Sports Lawyer* 9:2 (Summer 1991), 34, 36 at notes 62, 72, 74.

43. *Ward, et al. v. Rock Against Racism* 109 S. Ct. 2746 (1989).

44. Adam M. Kanzer, "Misfit Power, the First Amendment and the Public Forum: Is There Room in America for the Grateful Dead?" *Columbia Journal of Law and Social Problems* 25:3 (1992), 521–565.

45. John Seabrook, "The World of Television, Rocking in Shangri-La," *The New Yorker* (Oct. 10, 1994), 64–78.

3

Two Perspectives on Ice-T: "Can't Touch Me": Musical Messages and Incitement Law

Sandra Davidson

Guns! The very word strikes terror even in corporate hearts—or perhaps embarrassment or anger. Gangsta rappers have felt the heat of corporate displeasure and of the law. Nonrappers have taken corporate hits, as well. For instance, Sheryl Crow, a Grammy winner, felt the brunt of Wal-Mart's wrath in the fall of 1996 when the chain refused to sell her album containing the song "Love Is a Good Thing." Maybe love is a good thing, but these lyrics were a *bad* thing, according to Wal-Mart. The lyrics said children were killing each other with guns from Wal-Mart.[1]

Wal-Mart thought the lyrics were unfair because the chain stopped selling handguns in stores in 1994 after being sued by relatives of a couple killed by their son. He purchased his gun at Wal-Mart, even though the federal form he filled out indicated he had received treatment for mental problems. (Handguns are still available through Wal-Mart's catalogs.) Because Wal-Mart is the only outlet for music in many small communities, the refusal to sell Crow's albums resulted in an estimated loss of 400,000 sales.[2]

Crow did not advocate violence. Quite the contrary. But Rap stars Ice-T and the late Tupac Shakur produce music that arguably glorifies violence. The question is whether it *incites* violence. Incitement could even result in court judicial intervention, but the First Amendment places a high hurdle for the government if it is to meet the U.S. Supreme Court's incitement standards. The First Amendment, however, cannot protect musicians from economic suppression.

HOLY SMOKE! BOYCOTT *BATMAN?*

Powerful companies such as Time-Warner are major players in the struggle for creative freedom for rappers. Time-Warner and Ice-T present an interesting case study. Perhaps they also reveal a double standard existing in the United States that's based on the race of the artists involved.

In 1992, Time-Warner produced the movie *Batman Returns* and met with no resistance. In 1992, Sire Records, a Time-Warner subsidiary, produced Ice-T's *Body Count* and the war on words began.[3] Both of these creative efforts had the potential to inflame.

"Burn, Baby, Burn," says Danny DeVito as his drooling, fish-breathed character, "Penguin," watches flames swallow Gotham City in *Batman Returns*.[4] Perhaps, in retrospect, "Burn, Baby, Burn" was an unfortunate choice of words. In a movie designed to be sheer escapist entertainment, Penguin echoes the chant from the 1965 Watts riots in Los Angeles.[5] In 1991, Los Angeles burned again after the acquittal of police officers who beat Rodney King while a videocamera recorded their blows. *Batman Returns* was already well into production before the second burning of Los Angeles. And Rap-singer Ice-T recorded his album *Body Count* before the reburning. Almost a year before the second Los Angeles conflagration, Ice-T says, he recorded his song, "Cop Killer."[6]

Almost as predictable as the riots that resulted from the acquittal in the King beating case was the reaction of police officers to Ice-T's "Cop Killer" song. Law-enforcement associations in Texas and New York urged a boycott of Time-Warner products.[7]

On June 18, 1992, Ice-T wrapped himself in the cloak of the First Amendment and defended his album, to the approval of the crowd in New York City at the 13th annual New Music Seminar. "What they're really trying to do," Ice-T told the crowd about the police, "is shut down my platform. They do not want to let me be able to speak to the masses."[8] He views his message as one of anti-racism: "The enemies on that album are racist people—the KKK—parents, no matter what race you are—if you teach racism to your kids—and brutal police."[9]

The unrepentant rapper asked, "If the cops got a problem with me, why don't they move on me? Because they can't touch me. They can't boycott me. They don't buy my records anyway. So they know they cannot possibly touch me without killing me."[10] Ice-T also used his they'll-have-to-kill-me-to-shut-me-up theme in saying, "They're going to have to lay cross hairs on me and do me, because I will not stop telling the truth . . . If they lock me up, I'm going to keep doing it from a cell."[11]

THE SUPREME COURT'S INCITEMENT STANDARD

The chances of Ice-T being locked in a cell for his lyrics were nil. Since its first attempt to interpret the First Amendment in 1919 in *Schenck v. United States*,[12] the U.S. Supreme Court has progressed from a nebulous "clear and present danger" test to a position more like that expressed by John Stuart Mill. In 1859 in his book *On Liberty*, Mill wrote that "even opinions lose their immunity, when the circumstances in which they are expressed are such as to constitute their expression a positive instigation to some mischievous act."[13] As of 1969, when the U.S. Supreme Court decided *Brandenburg v. Ohio*,[14] an "incitement" standard has prevailed to protect expression. In *Brandenburg*, the Court decreed, "[C]onstitutional guarantees of free speech and free press do not permit a State to forbid . . . advocacy of the use of force or of law violation except where advocacy is directed to inciting or producing imminent lawless action and is likely to incite or produce such actions."[15] What does this mean to rappers such as Ice-T? In a word, *freedom*. Mere advocacy of a violation of a law, such as cop killing, may not be punished. More is required. First, the advocacy must be "directed to inciting or producing imminent lawless action." That is, the speaker's subjective intent must be to cause almost immediate cop killing. And second, the advocacy must be "likely to incite or produce such actions." In other words, there must be an objective likelihood of the speaker's success. The *Brandenburg* test also can be viewed as a three-part test, requiring intent, imminence, and likelihood. But the "incitement" standard under *Brandenburg* is an extremely high hurdle for someone seeking to suppress or punish speech. As the U.S. Court of Appeals for the Sixth Circuit correctly observed, "without actual incitement, First Amendment considerations argue against . . . liability."[16]

At a press conference held before Ice-T's speech to the New Music Seminar, he said, "At no point do I go out and say 'Let's do it.' I'm singing in the first person as a character who is fed up with police brutality."[17] Short of Ice-T's standing in front of a group of concert goers and purposely trying to work them into a frenzy to immediately "kill some cops," Ice-T appears safe from legal action.

ECONOMIC PRESSURE

Being safe from legal compulsion does not mean one is safe from social and economic pressure. In 1992, Peter Kehoe, the head of the New York State Sheriff's Association, predicted, "As a direct result of this song, cops will be killed during the upcoming hot summer months while Time-Warner executives sit beside their swimming pools . . . enjoying their ill-gotten gains."[18] Events have not borne out this prediction—there has been no wave of cop killings.

In its defense, Time-Warner released a statement saying that banning the record "will not make violence and rage disappear" and that Time-Warner stands by its "commitment to the free expression of ideas for all our authors, journalists, recording artists, screenwriters, actors and directors."[19] But Kehoe said, "It has nothing to do with freedom of expression. It has everything to do with incredible corporate greed, with incredible social irresponsibility and with an incredible lack of taste, discretion and sensitivity."[20]

Clearly, heads of police organizations were alarmed. The president of the 8,000-member Los Angeles police union, Bill Violante, opined, "The publication of such vile trash is unconscionable. This song does nothing but arouse the passions of the criminal element who make the streets of Los Angeles unsafe." And the president of the 230,000-member Fraternal Order of Police, Paul Taylor, warned, "People who ride around all night and use crack cocaine and listen to rap music that talks about killing cops—it's bound to pump them up. No matter what anybody tells you, this kind of music is dangerous."[21]

Two police organizations and local politicians in Los Angeles demanded that Time-Warner voluntarily quit distributing "Cop Killer." In Alabama, the governor called the record's lyrics "obscene."[22] Actor Charlton Heston and 60 members of Congress also denounced Ice-T.[23] In response to such pressure, Super Club Music, Inc., which is based in Atlanta, promised to pull the album from its shelves in more than 300 stores in 19 states.[24] And Trans World Music of Albany, N.Y., also promised to pull the album from its 600 stores across the nation. Sales of the album soared to a half million in stores still stocking it. Still, in July 1992, Ice-T bowed to the pressure and agreed to withdraw "Cop Killer" from his *Body Count* album.[25] However, he vowed to distribute the song for free at his concerts.[26] The new album, minus "Cop Killer," sold nearly as many copies as the original version.[27] Ice-T and Time-Warner parted company in 1993,[28] and in September 1994, Ice-T and Virgin Records released an album, *Born Dead*, which has no allusions to killing cops. One commentator said "Brain Dead" would have been a better title,[29] and another said "Born Dead" was stillborn.[30] Ice-T blames MTV for the failure of the album to sell well because, according to Ice-T, MTV did not play his "two decent videos."[31]

Ice-T has not been the only black rap artist getting heat. On June 13, 1992, speaking to Rev. Jesse Jackson's Rainbow Coalition, then-Democratic presidential candidate Bill Clinton criticized Sister Souljah for saying, "If black people kill black people every day, why not have a week and kill white people?"[32] Clinton even compared her comments to those made by former KKK-member David Duke.[33] Three days later, in response to criticisms of his remarks, Clinton said on MTV, "It is never right . . . particularly for people of influence to say there are no good people of another race, that maybe all the blacks should go kill whites for a change."[34]

"Basically, they're after all of us," Ice-T said. "Say something that's not just straight down the line . . . and they're coming to get you."[35] Ice-T has a point. When—if ever—should we as a society censor him?[36] Sister Souljah? Tupac Shakur?

"Cop Killer" certainly isn't the first song about killing authorities. "I Shot the Sheriff," by Bob Marley, is a 1970s song. No record company pulled it. But, in the wake of the "Cop Killer" controversy, A & M Records did ask rapper Tragedy to pull his song about a police shooting, "Bullet," from his *Black Rage* album. Hollywood Basic, before it released the album *Rumors of a Dead Man* by Samoan rap group Boo-Yaa Tribe, required the group to pull "Shoot 'Em Down." Warner asked the group Juvenile Committee to redo its song "Justice for the Head" by deleting a reference to cop killing. Warner refused to distribute the album *Live and Let Die* by Kool G Rap and DJ Polo.[37] And Warner also refused to let its Tommy Boy subsidiary release the album *Bush Killa* by rapper Paris.[38] Although not censoring gangsta rapper MC Eiht's *We Come Strapped* album, in 1994, Epic Records, a division of Sony, slapped a label on it saying, "The lyrical content contained on this album solely expresses the views of the artist." The album contains a song, "Take 2 Wit Me," about a drug dealer who kills two police officers.[39]

CONGRESS HAD HEARINGS, BUT TOOK NO ACTION

Compulsion and labels came only from protesters[40] and the record companies, not from legislators. Legislators held hearings in Washington, D.C., but have not introduced legislation. On February 11, 1994, in the wake of an NAACP "outreach" conference at the nation's capital, the House Subcommittee on Commerce, Consumer Protection, and Competitiveness held hearings on rap lyrics. No calls for legislation resulted.[41]

Then on February 23, 1994, the Senate Juvenile Justice Subcommittee held hearings on gangsta rap, summoning executives and performers from the rock-music industry, social scientists, and child violence experts. Senator Carol Moseley-Braun, a Democrat from Illinois, convened the Senate hearings.[42] Singer Dionne Warwick called gangsta rap "pornographic," while MTV's Nicholas Butterworth defended gangsta rap as an icon for the violence and unemployment of this era the way protest music was for the Vietnam War era.[43] The only rapper to testify was Errol James.[44] The Subcommittee Chairman, Herbert Kohl, a Democrat from Wisconsin, suggested that the music industry rate music the way the movie industry rates movies, and Moseley-Braun also asked for more responsibility from the industry.[45] But no calls for legislation from the House or Senate resulted from this hearing.[46]

On May 5, 1994, after a second wave of hearings, Representative Cardiss Collins, a Republican from Illinois, said no legislation to prevent sales of gangsta rap to minors would result.[47] None did.

RECORD LABELING: A VOLUNTARY ENDEAVOR

Although gangsta rap precipitated the latest, futile call for mandatory record labeling, the first call for labeling originated in 1983 when Tipper Gore, wife of then-Senator Al Gore, heard one of her children playing a song by Prince, "Darling Nikki." Tipper Gore was incensed. "Darling Nikki," it seems, was doing something in a hotel lobby with a magazine that the magazine's publisher probably hadn't intended.[48] The next year, 1985, she and Susan Baker, wife of then-Secretary of the Treasury James Baker, formed the Parents' Music Resource Center (PMRC). The group pressed for record labeling and for congressional hearings on sexually explicit and violent lyrics.[49] That same year, congressional hearings were held before the Senate Commerce, Science and Transportation Committee.   Senator Gore happened to be on that committee.[50] Frank Zappa livened up the hearings, testifying in opposition to labeling and calling Tipper Gore a "cultural terrorist."[51]

Also in 1985, bowing to pressure from both Gore's group and the congressional hearings, the Recording Industry Association of America (RIAA) agreed to place, voluntarily, warning labels on records.[52] The RIAA represents most of the major record companies in the United States.[53]

The voluntary labeling, however, was not enough to satisfy some state legislators. With songs such as "Bodily Dismemberment" by Rigor Mortis and "Me So Horny" by 2-Live Crew out there for young ears to hear, labeling legislation was prepared in

1990 in at least a dozen states[54]—maybe as many as 18.[55] In 1989, hoping to ward off legislation, the RIAA had decided to standardize its labeling.

In 1990, labeling legislation passed only in Louisiana, and Governor Buddy Roemer vetoed it.[56] In 1990,[57] a bill introduced by Republican Jean Dixon in the Missouri state legislature would have required record labels with black letters on a yellow florescent background saying "PARENTAL ADVISORY" and "WARNING": "May contain explicit lyrics descriptive of or advocating one or more of the following: nudity, Satanism, suicide, sodomy, incest, beastiality, sadomasochism, adultery, murder, morbid violence, or any deviate sexual conduct in a violent context, or the . . . illegal use of drugs or alcohol."[58] Dixon received a lot of publicity, appearing, for instance, on National Public Radio's "Morning Edition" and on Cable News Network's "Crossfire."[59] But the bill failed to pass, and Dixon did not get re-elected.[60]

But in 1992, the state of Washington passed legislation that would have permitted prosecutors to ask judges to find that particular records offend community standards and appeal to the prurient interests of children. Those records then would have to be labeled "adults only," and dealers who did not restrict the sales of such albums could have been fined $500 and jailed for six months on a first offense, and fined up to $5,000 and jailed for one year for subsequent offenses.[61] But only five months after this "erotic music" law went into effect, a state judge struck it down as a violation of free speech. The judge believed that the law, which offered no method of informing record retailers that a record had been found obscene, would have had a chilling effect on speech.[62]

On October 21, 1992, Al Gore appeared on MTV for a 90-minute "town hall" meeting. His grilling included half-a-dozen questions about record labeling. He defended labeling as an appropriate method of protecting children, but he also said, "I'm totally opposed to censorship, and I might say Tipper is as well. We're both former journalists, and we believe in the First Amendment.[63]

Tipper Gore resigned from the PMRC in 1993, saying that its "work was done."[64] Speaking of the PMRC, she said, "We are only in favor of voluntary labeling."[65] Some artists have taken up voluntary labeling. For instance, in 1992, Prince, whose song "Darling Nikki" got Tipper Gore interested in labeling, released his "rock soap opera."[66] He did two versions—one with a warning label, one without. He cleaned up his song "Sexy MF" for the unlabeled version. Instead of using a beep tone, he used a scream to replace the offensive word.[67] His label (Paisley Park/Warner Brothers) wanted as wide a distribution of the record as possible, and some conservative record stores refuse to stock records with the warning labels.[68] And 2-Live Crew released *As Clean as They Wanna Be*, an album that sold only one-tenth as many copies as their earlier album, *As Nasty as They Wanna Be*.[69] Ironically, both albums got the group in legal trouble, but 2-Live Crew prevailed in a copyright suit over their parody of Roy Orbison's "Pretty Woman" in their *Clean* album[70] as well as obscenity charges for their *Nasty* album.[71]

Truly voluntary acts, such as labeling, do not carry the sting that government labeling would. And titles such as "Cop Killer" seem to be a form of self-labeling, announcing that a work contains violence.

CIVIL SUITS HAVE FAILED—SO FAR

A civil suit is another mode of suppressing expression that requires the cooperation of the court system, but it is essentially driven by private individuals. In a civil suit, the plaintiff has the burden of proving the case by a "preponderance of the evidence." This is a much lower standard of proof than in a criminal prosecution, where a prosecutor must prove guilt "beyond a reasonable doubt." But even with this lower burden of proof, civil litigants have not yet won suits against rockers or rappers.

Rock stars and their record companies prevailed in suits alleging that their music led to suicides. Ozzy Osbourne won two such suits. In 1991, in *Waller v. Osbourne*,[72] parents sued Osbourne and his record company in Georgia, claiming their son shot himself after listening repeatedly to the song, "Suicide Solution." The parents sought $9 million in damages,[73] contending the music "incites imminent lawless action." But the federal district court made clear that under the *Brandenburg* test, the music would lose its First Amendment protection only if it were "directed to inciting or producing imminent lawless action and is likely to incite or produce such action."[74] The court concluded that the music did not constitute "culpable incitement."[75] The U.S. Court of Appeals for the Eleventh Circuit affirmed the district court's decision,[76] and in 1992 the Supreme Court let the lower courts' decisions stand.[77] Osbourne likewise prevailed in an earlier suit, *McCollum v. CBS*,[78] brought in 1988 by parents of another child who had committed suicide after listening to the same song.

In 1990, a judge in Nevada dismissed a similar suit against rock star Judas Priest involving a 1985 suicide allegedly prompted by the album *Stained Class*.[79]

The music of the late Tupac Shakur came under fire in a civil suit brought by widow Linda Davidson. Her husband, Bill, a 43-year-old state trooper and father of two, was shot to death on April 11, 1992, when he stopped 18-year-old motorist, Rodney Ray Howard, who was speeding down a Texas highway near Aurora in a stolen Chevrolet Blazer blaring rap music. The trooper stopped him because of a missing headlight.[80] At the time of the shooting, Howard was listening to "2pacalypse Now" by Tupac (or 2pac) Amaru Shakur, with inflammatory lyrics.[81]

Because of pretrial publicity, Howard's murder case was moved from Jackson County (site of the shooting) to Austin County.[82] During the trial, Howard's lawyer, Allen Tanner, tried to prove that the music influenced Howard, describing him as a "rap addict who lived, breathed and worshiped" the life-style depicted in gangsta rap. Hoping the jury would get a feel for the music enjoyed by Howard, Tanner played gangsta rap for the jurors—by Shakur, Geto Boys, Ice Cube, Ganksta N-I-P, and N.W.A.[83] Tanner played songs such as "City Under Siege," "Money and the Power," "Trigger Happy Police," and "Slaughter."[84]

During his murder trial, Howard testified that listening to Shakur's music gave him "a fight-back attitude versus stay away."[85] And District Attorney Robert E. Bell repeatedly told the jury that he hated gangsta rap, but that it should not be a mitigating factor.[86]

The jury convicted Howard of murder on June 8, 1993.[87] The jury deliberated for approximately half an hour over his guilt.[88] On July 14, 1993, the jury sentenced 19-

year-old Howard to die.[89] The jurors deliberated for five days over his sentence,[90] twice returning notes to the judge saying they were deadlocked.[91]

Widow Linda Davidson sued Shakur, Interscope Records, and its parent company, Time-Warner.[92] Her lawyer, James Cole of Victoria, Texas,[93] removed the case from state court to the U.S. District Court for the Southern District of Texas.[94] The case had been set for trial on October 23, 1995,[95] but the defense moved for summary judgment, and the case was removed from the trial docket.[96] In its motion for summary judgment, the defense was saying, in effect, that there is no disagreement between the plaintiff and defense on the facts of the case. Further, given these facts, the defense must win based on the law. In March 1997, the judge ruled in favor of Tupac Shakur and Time-Warner.[97]

Why had the widow sued? The "goal" in filing the $100 million suit against Time-Warner, the plaintiff's attorney said, was "to punish Time-Warner and wake up the executives who run the music business." He continued, "It is time giant corporations were stopped from shameless making money off music designed to incite impressionable young men to shoot and kill cops."[98]

The suit claimed the "music contained on the tape was directed to inciting young black males, including Rodney Howard, to kill policemen. The incitement was directed to and resulted in imminent action."

The suit also alleged negligence and gross negligence in producing and selling the music.[99] In short, it was also a products liability suit.[100] Three theories were present in the suit—incitement, negligence, and products liability.[101] Under an incitement theory, plaintiffs must prove intent.[102] Under a negligence theory, plaintiffs must show, among other elements, foreseeability of the harm.[103] But under a products liability theory, a plaintiff can win under the doctrine of strict liability, meaning that if the plaintiff can prove that the product caused the harm, the producer can be liable regardless of intent or negligence.[104]

The suit presented the anomaly of Linda Davidson not wanting the music to be a mitigating factor in Howard's capital murder case, but wanting the makers of the music to be found civilly liable for the murder.[105]

While the suit was still pending, on Friday, September 13, 1996, Tupac Shakur died.[106] His bad luck had come in Las Vegas six days before, when he was shot four times in the chest.[107] Shakur's life had been plagued by gunfire. On October 31, 1993, he had been charged with wounding two off-duty police officers who were shot in Atlanta,[108] but he was not convicted.[109] And on November 30, 1994, he had been shot five times in the groin.[110]

THE BOTTOM LINE

The bottom line is that the First Amendment protects Ice-T and other rappers from censorship by the government. "Incitement" is difficult for prosecutors because they must prove three elements beyond a reasonable doubt: intent, imminence, and likelihood. In the legal sense, Ice-T is right—"can't touch me." But while rappers can't be touched by prosecutors, they are not free from social and economic pressure.

Corporations, pressured by individuals who threaten boycotts, can slow rappers down by pulling support from them. Stores can refusef to stock albums.

Civil suits threaten to touch rockers and rappers in the pocketbook. So far, however, individuals have not prevailed in suits against rockers or rappers. But a suit against the late Tupac Shakur has survived his death. Suits become another form of economic pressure because even when rappers win, suits are expensive to defend.

In sum, the First Amendment gives important but narrow protection to rappers; the government could only stop music that truly incited violence. But the First Amendment has no effect on corporations or individuals who apply economic pressure on rappers.

NOTES

1. "Wal-Mart Bans Album because of Gun Lyrics," *The Houston Chronicle*, 3 Star Edition, Sept. 10, 1996, p. 3; Reuters World Service, BC cycle, September 10, 1996.

2. "Wal-Mart Bans Album because of Gun Lyrics."

3. Barry Layne, "Angry Rapper Ice-T: 'Cops Should Feel Threatened,'" BPI Entertainment News Wire, June 20, 1992; Irwin Arieff, "Quayle Hits Time-Warner Over Rap Singer Ice-T," Reuters, June 19, 1992, AM cycle.

4. Ben Macintyre, "Police Press for Boycott of Batman Film over Cop Killer Song," *The Times*, Overseas News (June 19, 1992).

5. Ibid.

6. Richard Roth, "Cop-Killing Rap Lyrics Are a Subject of Controversy," CNN News, Transcript # 60–5, June 19, 1992; Richard Roth, "Ice-T Addresses New Music Seminar on 'Cop Killer' CD," CNN, "Showbiz Today," Transcript # 69–1, June 18, 1992; David Treadwell, "Ice-T Rips Efforts to Suppress His 'Cop Killer' Song," *Los Angeles Times*, Home Edition, June 19, 1992, p. F1.

7. AP, "Rapper Ice-T Defends Song Against Spreading Boycott," *New York Times*, Late Edition-Final, June 19, 1992, p. C24. The 35,000 members of the National Black Politic Association did not join in the boycott. "Uh-huh, You Had the Right One, Baby," *Chicago Tribune*, North Sports Final Edition, June 18, 1992, p. 24.

8. Treadwell, "Ice-T Rips Efforts."

9. Roth, "Cop-Killing Rap Lyrics"; Roth, "Ice-T Addresses."

10. Roth, "Ice-T Addresses."

11. Layne, "Angry Rapper Ice-T."

12. *Schenck v. United States*, 249 U.S. 47 (1919).

13. John Stuart Mill, *On Liberty*, Part III. In Max Lerner, ed., *Essential Works of John Stuart Mill* (New York: Bantam Books, 1961), p. 304.

14. *Brandenburg v. Ohio*, 395 U.S. 44 (1969).

15. *Brandenburg v. Ohio*, 395 U.S. 447. In *Brandenburg*, a Ku Klux Klan leader was convicted of violating a statute prohibiting advocacy of "the duty, necessity, or propriety of sabotage, violence or unlawful methods of terrorism as a means of accomplishing industrial or political reform." *Brandenburg v. Ohio*, 395 U.S. 444–445. The proscription of "*unlawful* methods of terrorism" of course raises the question of whether there are *lawful* methods of terrorism.

16. *Watters v. TSR, Inc.*, 904 F.2d 378, 383 (6th Cir. 1990).

17. AP, "Rapper Ice-T Defends Song"; Layne, "Angry Rapper Ice-T."

18. Macintyre, "Police Press for Boycott."

19. Treadwell, "Ice-T Rips Efforts."

20. Roth, "Ice-T Addresses."

21. Chuck Phillips, "Police Groups Urge Halt of Record's Sale," *Los Angeles Times*, Home Edition, June 16, 1992, p. F1.

22. Roth, "Ice-T Addresses."

23. Neil Strauss, "The Pop Life," *New York Times*, Late Edition-Final, May 25, 1994, p. 17C.

24. "Ice-T Meltdown Begins," *Chicago Tribune*, North Sports Final Edition, June 19, 1992, p. 24, zone C; AP, "Rapper Ice-T Defends Song"; Treadwell, "Ice-T Rips Efforts."

25. Deborah Tannen, "He Said, She Said: What You Say, How You Say It: It Takes Work to Understand," *San Diego Union-Tribune*, Dec. 26, 1994, p. E-1.

26. "The Best of 1992," *op. cit.*; Greg Kot, "Chilling Silence: Shhhh! Listen Carefully for the Sound of Censors," *Chicago Daily Tribune*, Final Edition, Dec. 27, 1992, p. 12.

27. Deborah Tannen, "He Said, She Said."

28. Ibid.

29. Rick Mitchell, "Public Enemy Calls to Action," *The Houston Chronicle*, 2 Star Edition, Sept. 4, 1994, p. 6. See also, Ed Murrieta, "Ice T, Foes Ready to Rock 'n' Roll Again," *Sacramento Bee*, Metro Final, May 25, 1994, p. A2.

30. Deborah Tannen, "He Said, She Said."

31. "Entertainment Summary," *Reuters*, BC cycle, Dec. 21, 1994.

32. Macintyre, "Police Press for Boycott."

33. Chuck Phillips, "'I Do Not Advocate . . . Murdering'; 'Raptivist' Sister Souljah Disputes Clinton Charge," *Los Angeles Times*, Home Edition, June 17, 1992, p. F1.

34. Macintyre, "Police Press for Boycott." For commentary, see, e.g., Gregory Freeman, "Clinton Gets a Bad Rap," *St. Louis Post-Dispatch*, June 19, 1992, p. C1.

35. Treadwell, "Ice-T Rips Efforts."

36. For commentaries with differing views, see, Michael Kinsley, "Ice-T: Is the Issue Social Responsibility . . . " and Barbara Ehrenreich, " . . . Or Is It Creative Freedom?" *Time*, July 20, 1992, pp. 88–89.

37. Kot, "Chilling Silence."

38. Amy Linden, Tony Scherman, and David Hiltbrand, "Picks & Pans" section, *People*, Jan. 11, 1993, p. 21.

39. Richard Harrington, "Beyond the Parental Advisory; Sony's Epic Label Adds a Disclaimer Sticker of Its Own," *Washington Post*, Final Edition, July 27, 1994, p. D7.

40. For an article on protests against gangsta rap by the National Political Congress of Black Women, see Catherine Applefeld, "Group Battles Gangsta Rap; Women Barricade D.C. Wiz Store," *Billboard*, Jan. 8, 1994, p. 3.

41. Bill Holland, "NAACP Joins in Anti-Gangsta Fray; Md. Chapter's Statement Calls for Hearings," *Billboard*, Feb. 26, 1994, p. 6.

42. Paul Basken, "Rock Music Industry Before Congress," UPI, BC cycle, Feb. 23, 1994.

43. Brooks Boliek, "Senate Probes Gangsta Rap: Porno or Poetry?" BPI Entertainment News Wire, Feb. 25, 1994.

44. Linda M. Harrington, "On Capitol Hill, a Real Rap Session; Mean Lyrics Blamed on the Mean Streets," *Chicago Tribune*, North Sports Final Edition, Feb. 24, 1994, p. 1, Zone N.

45. Michael Posner, "Groups Fight over Regulating 'Gangsta Rap,'" *Reuters*, BC cycle, Feb. 23, 1994.

46. Holland, "NAACP Joins in Anti-Gangsta Fray"; Boliek, "Senate Probes Gangsta Rap."

47. Irv Lichtman, "The Billboard Bulletin," *Billboard*, May 14, 1994, p. 110.

48. Linda Stasi, Doug Vaughan, and Anthony Scaduto, "Inside New York," *Newsday*, Jan. 17, 1993, p. 11.

49. Gene Seymour, "In the Current Climate, What You See and Hear Is Not Always What the Artist, Film Maker or Songwriter Had in Mind," *Newsday*, May 20, 1990, p. 14.

50. Tara Parker Pope, "Campaign '92: Clinton Chooses Gore; Can Tipper Gore Neutralize GOP on Values Issue?" *The Houston Chronicle*, 2 Star Edition, July 10, 1992, p. 16.

51. Dave Lesher, "'92 Democratic Convention; Will Tipper Gore's Values Strike Home?" *Los Angeles Times*, Home Edition, July 15, 1992, p. 7A.

52. Richard Harrington, "The New Wave of Lyrics Laws; Listening to Both Sides of the Record-Labeling Debate," *The Washington Post*, Final Edition, Jan. 28, 1990, p. G1.

53. "National Editorial Sampler; What Newspapers are Saying," UPI, Aug. 23, 1985, BC cycle.

54. Harrington, "New Wave of Lyrics Laws."

55. Bill Holland, "Assault on 1st Amendment Stirred Industry to Action," *Billboard*, Jan. 5, 1991, "1990 in Review" section, p. 7; Eric Snider, "Tipper Got a Bad Rap," *St. Petersburg Times*, Oct. 6, 1992, p. 2D.

56. Holland, "Assault on 1st Amendment."

57. House Bill 1406. Wendy Hickey, "Stamp of Disapproval," *Columbia Daily Tribune*, March 18, 1990, p. 35.

58. House Bill 1406 (1990). Of all the bills introduced on record labeling, Dixon's bill "has perhaps the widest reach of all," commented Richard Harrington, "New Wave of Lyrics Laws."

59. Rudi Keller, "In the Limelight," *Columbia Daily Tribune*, Feb. 24, 1990, p. 1.

60. "Most Incumbents Renominated: Rep. Jean Dixon Loses in Springfield Re-election Bid," *Columbia Daily Tribune*, Aug. 8, 1990, p. 11.

61. Chuck Philips, "Rock Industry Rapped for Inaction; Producer Decries Lyrics Law Response," *Los Angeles Times*, Home Edition, June 4, 1992, Calendar section, p. F1; Chris Morris, "Judge Bars Enforcing of Wash.'s Erotic Music Law," *Billboard*, Nov. 14, 1992, Artists & Music section, p. 10. House Bill 2554. Phillips, "Rock Industry Rapped." It was an amendment to an "erotic materials" law that had been in effect in Washington since 1969. Richard Harrington, "Labeling Law Struck Down," *Washington Post*, Final Edition, Nov. 4, 1992, p. C7.

62. Morris, "Judge Bars"; Harrington, "Labeling Law Struck Down."

63. Susan Page, "Campaign Countdown; 12 Days," *Newsday*, Nassau and Suffolk Edition, Oct. 22, 1992, p. 18.

64. Susan Milligan, "Deadhead Tipper Shows She's No Iceberg; Second Lady's Actions Belie Prudish Image Gained in Rock War," *The Phoenix Gazette*, Final, April 7, 1994, p. A1; Susan Milligan, "Same Old Tipper—Only Her Press Has Changed," *St. Louis Post-Dispatch*, Three Star Edition, April 3, 1994, p. 2B.

65. Ibid. For more on Tipper Gore's views, see *Raising PG Kids in an X-Rated Society*, (New York City: Bantam Doubleday Dell Publications, 1988). Pope, "Campaign '92 "; Lesher, "'92 Democratic Convention."

66. Jim Sullivan, "Prince of Raunchy Music," *The Boston Globe*, Oct. 13, 1992, p. 57.

67. "Happy Couple Takes the Plunge," *Chicago Tribune*, North Sports Final Edition, April 19, 1992, p. 24.

68. Sullivan, "Prince of Raunchy Music."

69. Brian Boyd, "Street Legal," *The Irish Times*, City Edition, July 29, 1994, p. 8.

70. See *Campbell v. Acuff-Rose Music, Inc.*, 510 U.S. 569 (1994).

71. See *Luke Records, Inc. v. Navarro*, 960 F.2d 134 (11th Cir. 1992). Also see Jeffrey L. L. Stein's chapter, "Music Lyrics: As Legally Censored as They Wanna Be," in this book.

72. 763 F. Supp. 1144 (D.C. Ga. 1991).

73. Russell Shaw, "'Suicide' Suit Dismissed; Judge: Osbourne Song Not Culpable," *Billboard*, May 18, 1991, p. 8.

74. 763 F. Supp. 1150 (quoting *Brandenburg*, 395 U.S. 447).

75. 763 F. Supp. 1151.

76. *Waller v. Osbourne*, 958 F.2d 1084 (11th Cir. 1992).

77. *Waller v. Osbourne*, 113 S. Ct. 325 (1992).

78. 212 Cal. App. 3d 989, 249 Cal Rptr. 187 (1988).

79. Shaw, "'Suicide' Suit Dismissed." See also Peter D. Csathy, "Takin' the Rap: Should Artists be Held Accountable for the Violent Recorded Speech?" 10 *Communications Lawyer* 7 (Spring 1992). The next target for suits may be country music, some commentators think. David Gelman, "Beware of Those Tears in Your Beers," *Newsweek*, Nov. 23, 1992, p. 90; Shirley Ragsdale, "Ragsdale: Is Suicide Country Music's New Dance Partner?" *Gannett News Service*, Dec. 22, 1992. A study that lasted a year and looked at 49 metropolitan areas led two sociologists to conclude that the greater the radio time devoted to country music, the higher the suicide rates for white listeners.

80. See, e.g., Yumi Wilson, "Back Beat of Pain and Anger in Music: Death Metal, Gangsta Rap, Grunge Rock Have a Common Theme," *San Francisco Chronicle*, May 31, 1994, Final Edition, p. E1; Chuck Philips, "Rap Defense Doesn't Stop Death Penalty; 'The Music Affected Me,' Says Ronald Ray Howard. 'That's How It Was that Night I Shot the Trooper,'" July 15, 1993, *Los Angeles Times*, Home Edition, p. F1; Sylvia Moreno, "Stakes High in Murder by Rap Fan; Trial Questions about 1st Amendment," *The Dallas Morning News*, June 21, 1993, Home Final Edition, p. 1A; Geordie Greig, "American Widow Sues for 'Murder Under the Influence of Rap,'" *Sunday Times*, Oct. 25, 1992.

81. Philips, "Rap Defense."

82. Janet Elliott, "When PR Sits Second Chair; 'Spin' Purveyors' Influence Grows at Major Texas Trials," *Tex. Law.*, Aug. 2, 1993, p. 1.

83. Philips, "Rap Defense."

84. Moreno, "Stakes High."

85. Elliott, "Killer's Sentence Sets Stage."

86. Elliott, "When PR Sits Second Chair"; Elliott, "Killer's Sentence Sets Stage." Two teenagers who killed policeman William A. Robertson in Milwaukee in September 1994 claimed they planned the sniper attack "because of a Tupac Shakur record that talks about killing the police." See Chuck Philips, "Gangsta Rap: Did Lyrics Inspire Killing of Police?" *Los Angeles Times*, Home Edition, Oct. 17, 1994, p. F2. The two were convicted of murder. See David Doege, "Walker Intended to Kill, Jury Rules," *Milwaukee Journal Sentinel*, Dec. 8, 1995, p. 1.

87. Sylvia Moreno, "Man Guilty in Rap Slaying Case; Music's Influence to Be Used in Defense Against Death Penalty," *The Dallas Morning News*, June 9, 1993, Home Final Edition, p. 12B.

88. On June 9, 1993, *The Dallas Morning News* reported that jury deliberations lasted for 25 minutes. On June 21, *The Dallas Morning News* reported that deliberations lasted for 26 minutes. Then on July 15, *The Dallas Morning News* reported that deliberations lasted for 40 minutes. See Moreno, "Man Guilty in Rap Slaying Case"; Moreno, "Stakes High"; Moreno, "Man Given Death Penalty in Rap Case; Jury Took 5 Days to Make Sentence Recommendation," *The Dallas Morning News*, July 15, 1993, Home Final Edition, p. 1A.

89. Moreno, "Man Given Death Penalty."

90. Moreno, "Man Given Death Penalty." See also, Elliott, "When PR Sits Second Chair." (Moreno and Elliott reported that deliberation lasted five days.) The jury's decision was rendered on the sixth day, resulting in some reports that deliberations lasted six days. See Philips, "Rap Defense."

91. Sylvia Moreno, "Man Given Death Penalty"; Philips, "Rap Defense."

92. Moreno, "Stakes High"; Philips, "Rap Defense."

93. Elliott, "When PR Sits Second Chair"; Janet Elliott, "Slain Trooper's Family Seeks Damages from Rapper; Round 2 in 'Gangsta Rap' Case," *Legal Times*, July 26, 1993, p. 10.

94. Telephone interview with Tracy Thormahlen, James Cole's legal assistant, July 6, 1994.

95. Telephone interview with Tracy Thormahlen, James Cole's legal assistant, Feb. 7, 1995.

96. Telephone interview with Tracy Thormahlen, James Cole's legal assistant, Nov. 21, 1994.

97. *Davidson v. Time-Warner, Inc.*, No. V-94-6, slip op. (S.D. Tex. March 28, 1997).   For extended discussion, see Davidson, "Blood Money: When Media Expose Others to Risk of Bodily Harm," 19 *Hastings Communications and Entertainment Law Journal*, Winter 1997, at pp. 225–309.

98. Greig, "American Widow Sues." For more on this case, see Chuck Philips, "Testing the Limits; The Fatal Shooting of a Texas Trooper During a Routine Traffic Stop Sets up a Conflict over the Words in a Rap Song that May Wind Up . . . Testing the Limits," *Los Angeles Times*, Home Edition, Oct. 13, 1992, p. F1; Chuck Philips, "Can We Blame Rap Lyrics?; Trooper's Death Renews Debate on Song Content," *The Houston Chronicle*, 2 Star Edition, Sept. 24, 1992, p. 1. Of course, Time-Warner has also been the center of controversy for the album *Body Count* by Ice-T. See, e.g., Greig, "American Widow Sues"; Peter D. Csathy, "Takin' the Rap: Should Artists Be Held Accountable for the Violent Recorded Speech?" 10 *Comm. Law.* 7 (Spring 1992); John Leland, "Rap and Race," *Newsweek*, June 29, 1992; AP, "Rapper Ice-T Defends"; Treadwell, "Ice-T Rips Efforts"; Chuck Philips, "Police Groups Urge Halt of Record's Sale," *Los Angeles Times*, Home Edition, June 16, 1992, p. F1. For commentary on the general subject of the effects of rap music, see Jason Talerman, "The Death of Tupac: Will Gangsta Rap Kill the First Amendment?" 14 *B.C. Third World L.J.* 117 (Winter 1994); Carol Kirschenbaum, "Is It a Bad Rap?" 14 *Austin Bus. J.* A1 (March 14, 1994); Jeffrey B. Kahan, "Bach, Beethoven and the (Home) Boys: Music History as it Ought to Be Taught," 66 *S. Cal. L. Rev.* 2583 (Sept. 1993); Roger Catlin, "Song Lyrics Reflect, Don't Cause Problems," *The Hartford Courant*, A Edition, July 6, 1992, p. A6.

99. Elliott, "Killer's Sentence Sets Stage."

100. Elliott, "When PR Sits Second Chair."

101. Telephone interview with Tracy Thormahlen, James Cole's legal assistant, July 6, 1994.

102. See *Brandenburg v. Ohio, supra* notes 195–98 and accompanying text.

103. See *McCollum v. CBS*, 202 Cal. App. 3d 989; 249 Cal Rptr. 187 (1988).

104. "Strict liability" imposes damages on the basis of "mere causation," regardless of whether a defendant was at fault. 491 U.S. at 547–48 (Justice White, dissenting).   Strict liability is often applied, for instance, to people who own wild animals. Under strict liability, if a person kept a tiger that got loose and killed another animal or a child, the person would not be asked whether he or she had been careful in trying to keep the tiger caged. The only question would be, "Is this your tiger?" If the person said "yes," the person would pay for the damage, regardless of whether he or she had been careful. For a discussion of *Florida Star*, see *supra* notes 81–91 and accompanying text.

105. Elliott, "When PR Sits Second Chair."

106. His death did not stop the suit against him, which proceeded against his estate. Telephone interview with Tracy Thormahlen, James Cole's legal assistant, Sept. 9, 1996. A study that lasted a year and looked at 49 metropolitan areas led two sociologists to conclude that the greater the radio time devoted to country music, the higher the suicide rates for white listeners. David Gelman, "Beware of Those Tears in Your Beers," *Newsweek*, Nov. 23, 1992, p. 90; Shirley Ragsdale, "Ragsdale: Is Suicide Country Music's New Dance Partner?" *Gannett News Service*, Dec. 22, 1992.

107. Robert Hilburn and Jerry Crow, "Rapper Tupac Shakur, 25, Dies 6 Days After Ambush," *Los Angeles Times*, Home Edition, Sept. 14, 1996, p. A1.   Shakur's death has

resulted in much commentary on the meaning of his life, his death, his music, and the rap-music industry. See, e.g., Johnnie L. Roberts, "Grabbing at a Dead Star," *Newsweek*, Sept. 1, 1997, p. 48; Connie Bruck, "The Takedown of Tupac," *The New Yorker* (July 7, 1997), p. 46; Jeff Leeds and Jim Newton, "FBI Probing Rap Label for Ties to Gangs, Drugs," *Los Angeles Times*, Orange County Edition, Sept. 29, 1996, p. 18A; Michel Marriott, "From Rap's Rhythms, a Retooling of Poetry," *The New York Times*, Late Edition Final, Sept. 29, 1996, p. 1; Cathy Maestri, "Drawing Lessons from a Rapper's Death," *The Press Enterprise* (Riverside, CA), Sept. 29, 1996, p. E03; Dana Kennedy, "Rap Wars; Did the Violence Claim Another Life?" *Entertainment Weekly*, Sept. 27, 1996, p. 8; J. D. Considine, "No Longer a War of Words," *The Fresno Bee*, Home Edition, Sept. 26, 1996, p. F3; David Van Biema, "'What Goes 'Round . . .'; Superstar Rapper Tupac Shakur Is Gunned Down in an Ugly Scene Straight out of His Own Lyrics," *Time*, Sept. 23, 1996, p. 40; Johnnie L. Roberts, "Blood on the Record Biz," *Newsweek*, Sept. 23, 1996, p. 69; Michael Eric Dyson, "The Culture Wars; Tupac: Living the Life He Rapped about in Song," *Los Angeles Times*, Home Edition, Sept. 22, 1996, p. 1M; Chrisena Coleman and Dave Saltonstall, "A Gangsta or Gangbusta? Rap World Debates Lessons of Shakur's Death," *Daily News* (New York), Sept. 22, 1996, p. 5; Esther Iverem, "Verses of Sorrow for Shakur; Rapper's Life Praised, Rebuked at Memorial," *Washington Post*, Final Edition, Sept. 22, 1996, p. D01.

108. See, e.g., "When Is Rap 2 Violent?" *Newsweek*, Nov. 29, 1993 (cover story: John Leland, "Gangsta Rap and the Culture of Violence," *Newsweek*, Nov. 29, 1993, p. 60); Kris Jensen, "Are Rap Rhymes and Crimes Connected?" *The Atlanta Journal and Constitution*, Nov. 23, 1993, p. D3 (citing Leland).

109. Tony Norman, "When Death Imitates Art," *Pittsburgh Post-Gazette*, Sooner Edition, Sept. 10, 1996, p. B-1.

110. "Rapper Tupac Shakur Robbed, Shot in N.Y.; Violence Marks Singer's Lyrics and Life," *Washington Post*, Final Edition, Dec. 1, 1994, p. A1. The very next day, a jury in Manhattan, New York, read its verdict that Shakur was "guilty" of sexually abusing a female fan; Shakur was absent. See Associated Press, "Shakur Found Guilty of Sex Abuse Charge," *Los Angeles Times*, Home Edition, Dec. 2, 1994, p. A31; "Wounded Rapper Convicted of Sex Abuse," *New York Times*, Late Edition, Dec. 2, 1994, p. B1. On February 7, 1995, Shakur received a sentence of up to four-and-a-half years. "Rapper Gets 4 ½ Years in Sex Case; Tupac Shakur Says He Did No Crime," *The Atlanta Journal and Constitution*, Feb. 8, 1995, p. B9; *Newsday*, "Rapper Shakur Sentenced to Prison in Sexual Assault," *The Houston Chronicle*, 2 Star Edition, Feb. 8, 1995, p. A8. He served eight months of his sentence and was out on bail when he was fatally shot. See Richard Roeper, "Rapper Shakur's Music an Ode to Gang Members," *Chicago Sun-Times*, Late Sports Final Edition, Sept. 11, 1996, p. 11; "Shakur Remains in ICU; No Leads Reported in Rapper's Shooting," *Washington Post*, Final Edition, Sept. 11, 1996, p. D08; Norman, "When Death Imitates Art."

4

The Politics of Aesthetic Response: Cultural Conservatism, the NEA, and Ice-T

David Slayden

By now, all that has to be said to provoke comment is "Ice-T." Everyone knows that he is a rapper and that he advocates killing cops in a song released in 1992 which, simply enough, is titled "Cop Killer." But the simplicity of the controversy ends with the literal reading of the song by the Combined Law Enforcement Associations of Texas (CLEAT), who saw it as an invocation to kill cops; acting on their reading of the lyrics, they called for a blanket boycott of Time-Warner, the parent company of Warner Bros. Records. CLEAT was reinforced by Governor Guy Hunt of Alabama, who demanded that record stores stop selling the album, *Body Count* (also the name of Ice-T's speed-metal band). Hunt's request was met by several national chains: Sound Warehouse, Super Club, and Trans World. In a letter to Time-Warner signed by 57 Republicans and 3 Democrats, Congress condemned the song, the artist, and the company. President Bush and Vice-President Quayle joined in the condemnation; Oliver North, not to be outdone, called for action, suggesting that charges of sedition be brought against Time-Warner. The commentary on "Cop Killer" by these public figures-turned-critics was enlivened by words typically associated with disease and the filth that spawns it, literal and figurative; the implication was quarantine.

The language directed toward Ice-T and his song was drawn from the vocabulary of repulsion: "sick," "obscene," "vile," "despicable," "ugly, destructive and disgusting." This is strong language for any reviewer, even critics of rock 'n' roll. But for cultural critics of the past decade working the trend of linking art, social agenda, and politics, it has pretty much become standard critical vocabulary. Although the stance taken and the message given by Ice-T rivals that of another notorious musical release, The Sex Pistols' "God Save the Queen," the reaction to "Cop Killer" plays not so much as a response to the shock of an attack on an authority figure as a directed effort to make good use of an opportunity to push an agenda.

The decrying of "Cop Killer" echoes the condemnation of the National Endowment for the Arts (NEA) since the early 1980s by those congressional watchdogs and citizen actions groups taking a protectionist and preservationist stance regarding American culture and American values. Regardless of one's judgment of the merits of Ice-T's work, several questions arise. Why such an official interest in culture, both commercial and noncommercial, in the past decade? When did culture become a political issue? And why is much of the discourse framed in terms that suggest the binary opposition of order and chaos linked in Matthew Arnold's *Culture and Anarchy* (1869)?[1]

This chapter examines the Ice-T controversy and relates it to the debates in the past decade over NEA funding of objectionable art works. Both of these incidents are expressions of the uncertainty regarding who or what defines culture—both high culture and mass culture—in postmodern America. The premise of this chapter is that postmodernism encompasses the variety of strategies now afoot, whose collective intention is not simply the questioning of the authority of the white, male author but a thorough dismantling of this voice as a habitually privileged source of meaning and value. This decentralizing characteristic of postmodernism creates anxieties of displacement, which mobilize reaction to contain and silence minority voices.

CULTURE AND CONFLICT

Lest the current buzzword status of "postmodern" further confuse an already confused issue, a historical analogue of culture and its invocation to play a role in ameliorating social conflict is instructive. Matthew Arnold wrote *Culture and Anarchy* in the wake of the Hyde Park Riots and offered culture as an antidote to the unruly masses, the disturbers if not the cause of the disturbance. He was addressing "the condition of England" question, a continuing problem of what to do about the increasingly visible and politically demanding masses populating the large industrial cities of Victorian England. As Arnold presents it, the problem was not so much that the masses lacked political representation or that they embraced the wrong culture; it was their lack of culture, which served, in Arnold's view, as a refining, controlling agent. The middle classes—the Barbarians—had failed to assume their charge as the arbiters of culture, so Arnold's call was to the ruling classes to once again rule as guardians of culture. "Sweetness and light" would prevail, and social order would result.

Arnold's analysis, in effect, dodges the issue of extending the franchise to the masses; such a strategy replaces a political issue with a cultural one and illegitimates any protest by the masses as an attack on national heritage. That the terms of our own current cultural debate are so similar suggests that the conditions are likewise comparable, that social change and the increased volume of previously silent or marginal voices constitutes a threat to values now construed as traditional by those opposed to change.

Traditional American values have been invoked in the decade-long scrutiny of the NEA by the amalgam of congressional representatives and citizens action groups against the public funding of obscene works; similar appeals to average American decency have fueled opposition to commercial cultural productions such as Ice-T's "Cop Killer." When on September 10, 1985, Representative Steve Bartlett (R-Texas) proposed an amendment prohibiting NEA grants from going to artists whose work is "patently offensive to the average person" and lacks "serious literary or artistic merit," he did so with the sense that he was defending a mainstream American public whose values were understood. (The amendment, however, was defeated because of a failure to define "average person" and "artistic merit."[2]) Jesse Helms, leader of the anti-NEA campaign in the U.S. Senate, stated the case more directly during the debate over the amendment bearing his name: "If senators want the Federal Government funding pornography, sadomasochism, or art for pedophiles, they should vote against my amendment."[3] It was a matter of good versus evil.

The logic of polarization characterizing Helm's rhetoric is dramatized by the alarmist stance taken up by Patrick Buchanan in a May 22, 1989, column in the *Washington Times*, asking if we are "Losing the War for America's Culture?"[4] Directing his wrath at Serrano's "Piss Christ," Buchanan quotes the warning given by Reagan in his farewell address: "[F]or those who create popular culture . . . patriotism is no longer in style." And Buchanan adds, "It was a dramatic understatement; America's art and culture are, more and more, openly anti-Christian, anti-American, nihilistic." The linkage of God and Country is assumed, as are the forces to which this combination is opposed. According to Buchanan, the American landscape is littered with irreligious, sexually deviant, and communist images. The reason? "While the right has been busy winning primaries and elections, cutting taxes and funding anti-communist guerrillas abroad, the left has been quietly seizing all the commanding heights of American art and culture." The antidote is a cultural counter-revolution. "Conservatives and the religious community that comprise the vast middle-American population should actively support those artists that advocate the same values and ideas they do. They should also choose to withdraw support and funding from the modernist culture they despise. In short, they should do what the liberals did long ago—'capture the culture.'"[5]

Although not exactly schooled in aesthetics, Buchanan understood his readers and appealed to them in two effective ways. First, his conceptualization of culture as a territory taken over by an undesirable other, by them, demands that "we" take it back. Second, he invokes "modernist culture," defined again through opposition; it is any art that does not advocate the same values and ideas "we" do. Beyond the we/them stance, the striking element of this rhetoric of cultural reclamation is the geographic character given to culture with the accompanying suggestion that a populist army will reclaim their rightful territory. This, in turn, recalls the basis for the neoconservative coalition opposing the production of immoral art supported by NEA grants; it was funded by the government—the people.

Whether government funding means government control has been an issue at least since 1981 when Reagan appointed the Presidential Task Force on the Arts and the Humanities to review the activities of the NEA and the National Endowment for the Humanities (NEH). Although the task force recommended maintaining the NEA's grant-giving structure, they also recommended strengthening the role of the Federal Council on the Arts and Humanities in overseeing the Endowment. This action suggested a revision, at least in spirit, of the government's role as stated in the National Foundation on the Arts and the Humanities Act of 1965, which created the Endowments. Public Law 89-209 states that "The practice of art and the study of humanities requires constant dedication and devotion and that, while no government can call a great artist or scholar into existence, it is necessary and appropriate for the federal government to help create and sustain not only a climate encouraging freedom of thought, imagination, and inquiry, but also the material conditions facilitating the release of this creative talent." In its report on the bill, the Senate Labor and Public Welfare Committee stresses that "fullest" attention be given "to freedom of artistic and humanistic expression. One of the artist's and humanist's great values to society is the mirror of self-examination which they raise so that society can become aware of its shortcomings as well as its strengths."[6]

Suggested in the Committee's report is the dialogic nature of art, that art engages society in a critique to which society responds through self-examination. It is precisely this dialogue that the conservative attacks on the NEA attempted to shut down. The retrospective "Robert Mapplethorpe: The Perfect Moment," or Andres Serrano's "Piss Christ" engaged in what conservatives labeled merely antisocial activity. Neoconservative art critic Hilton Kramer describes the controversial Mapplethorpe pictures as "the attempt to force upon the public the values of a sexual subculture that the public at large finds loathsome."[7] Furthermore, the justification of Mapplethorpe's or Serrano's work as cutting edge is absurd to Kramer, who characterizes the very idea of art now being cutting edge as "sentimentalization as well as a commercialization of the old idea of the avant-garde, which everyone knows no longer exists—except, possibly, in the realm of fashion design and advertising."[8]

Kramer's dismissal contradicts the concerns of conservative politicians and citizens action groups who saw evidence of a threatening progressive agenda in the controversial art. Although perhaps not avant-garde, certainly the art work that brought the NEA under attack represented minority voices, challenging traditional institutions of family, religion, and government with ideas of multiculturalism, feminism, and gay and lesbian rights. These were all causes or symptoms of social decay, according to Patrick Buchanan, who wrote: "A nation absorbs its values through its art. A corrupt culture will produce a corrupt people, and vice versa; between rotten art, films, plays and books—and rotten behavior—the correlation is absolute. The hour is late; America needs a cultural revolution in the '90s as sweeping as its political revolution in the '80s."[9]

Yet the cultural revolution called for by the right had a certain retro-fantasy quality, appealing to traditional values as a sort of code for eliminating diversity. In attacking the NEA, the right was seeking to control representations of gender, class, and race in the realm of high culture, erecting social boundaries by legitimizing and privileging one form of representation over another. It is not simply the silencing of voices but the dominance of a style, as in the case of protests against Chicago artist Erich Fischl's painting of a fully clothed boy looking at a naked man swinging at a baseball. Objections were raised against the painting "on the grounds that it promotes 'child molestation' and is, in any case, not 'realistic,' and therefore bad art."[10] In Norman Rockwell fashion, art is equated with realist representation but with a twist. Conceived in this way, art is a realistic rendering of a fixed notion of representation, of static, unchallenged social arrangements in support of the prevailing power structure. Official culture in a diverse society silences oppositional voices. The dialogue becomes a monologue.

The role of art and of the artist in culture has been hotly debated for some time, in both the art world and mass cultural productions. The argument that modernist dogma appears long ago to have abandoned any avant-garde claims and become an unwitting ally of the status quo is supported by the use of abstract expressionism in corporate architecture. In this context, nonrepresentational art serves as decoration, providing ambient color schemes rather than challenging preconceptions. Terrorist artists such as Robert Jones challenge the formalist notion put forward by critics like Clement Greenberg—that art exists in a vacuum. Jones asserts that all art is political, either by inclusion or exclusion. As he says, "Works of art become bodies with a certain magnetic personality or a certain gravity that radiates around them, so they do tend to pick up meanings."[11] This statement is in direct opposition to Greenberg's claim that avant-garde art is "too innocent . . . too difficult to inject effective propaganda into." The assertion that there is no pure realm of art separate from the exigencies of propaganda suggests that all forms of cultural expression—high art or mass culture—are subject to political meanings and uses. It further suggests the bias inherent in attempting to legislate taste by labeling one form of cultural expression as art and another as a criminal act by virtue of its content or medium. Once form is seen as inseparable from content, Ice-T fulfills Greenberg's expectation of the avant-garde's role by challenging assumptions and "keeping things moving during times of cultural rigor mortis."[12] Indeed, as with the debate between modern and postmodern theorists, the tension between art and politics provides much of the energy in Ice-T's music; that is why conservative coalitions find it to be "ugly, destructive and disgusting."

ART AS ENGAGEMENT

What the NEA controversies and the challenge to modernism have shown is the difficulty, if not impossibility, in separating aesthetics from politics, cultural representation from political representation. And what is further illustrated by the works at the center of the controversy is modernism's failure "to posit artworks as the products of an autonomous, disengaged form of labor and consumption, freed from normal, social commerce by virtue of their status as objects designed exclusively for visual pleasure."[13] Clearly, art is engaged. That the aesthetic categories of modernism were violated repeatedly by artistic production throughout the late 1960s and 1970s further emphasizes the degree to which such categories were socially and formally defined. The past 20 years have shown "significant crossovers between art and music, film and performance, sculpture and architecture, painting and popular culture."[14] This crossing over has blurred the boundaries between high culture and mass culture, but it has also altered the relationship of subcultures to the dominant culture. Whereas oppositional or marginal voices in the realm of high culture draw the scrutiny of a small number of government officials, increased cultural production in mass culture has made cultural products previously confined to a narrow sphere now available to a wide range of audiences. This commercial proliferation of cultural products further confuses distinctions between private and public space, creating anxieties over the production of meaning and the erasing of social boundaries.

As Richard Bolton has suggested, the NEA debates "were not really about funding but about how the public realm should be constituted."[15] The conservative agenda with the NEA was the creation of conformity through the silencing of oppositional voices. That the private realm is no less a contested area is evident in the controversy surrounding Ice-T. While the work of Mapplethorpe or Serrano can at least be posited as the output of recognized figures in the art world, Ice-T and his song "Cop Killer" comes without the sanction of a respected cultural association. The music is loud and fast and dominated by a heavy rhythm track. The lyrics are deliberately offensive; their speaker's stance is one of aggression and defiance. Ice-T is a rapper. "Cop Killer" is the output of his speed-metal band Body Count. Ice-T is young and male and commercially successful, and he is black.

Although Michael Jackson's conciliatory lyric says that it doesn't matter if you're black or white, in commercial culture, it does matter how you are black, particularly if you're a rap artist. Rap has an image problem. It is a music dominated, for the most part, by young black males, and this has impeded the chances for its artists to cross over into the mainstream of American culture. The majority of rap artists, not-withstanding the Fresh Prince, have eschewed the emasculation often deemed necessary for mainstream commercial success. Unlike Michael Jackson or Prince, their sexuality is not masked or ambiguous and their music is aggressive, outspoken, and often angry. In the media, to say "rap" is to say young, black, and male; it also suggests violence. This image accounts, in part, for the reporting of the controversy surrounding "Cop Killer," in which "rapper" Ice-T was repeatedly referenced. Yet "Cop Killer" is a rock song, Body Count is a speed-metal band, and the audience for the group is predominantly white suburban teenagers. Ice-T has repeatedly made this point. "I think by being rock it infiltrated the homes of a lot of parents not used to having their kids play records by rappers. They found out the music was made by a rapper. There is absolutely no way to listen to the song 'Cop Killer' and call it a rap record. It's so far from rap. But politically, they know by saying the word *rap* they can get a lot of people who think, 'Rap-black, rap-black-ghetto,' and don't like it."[16]

Rap as a musical form resists the usual effects of crossover. Its foregrounding of the rhythm, the lack of melody, the aggressive politics of the lyrics all defy attempts at covers. Thus, even though the fashions of hip-hop culture have become commercially viable, the core of rap remains fundamentally tied to its inner-city locale; the resistance of mainstream American culture to rap is directly analogous to the resistance to rock 'n' roll in the 1950s. Just as early rock 'n' roll records sent unacceptable messages to hitherto exclusive domains, rap artists, through venues such as "MTV Raps," are crossing cultural boundaries. Rap is accessible, and this is threatening. The congressional condemnation of Ice-T parallels action taken in 1954 by U.S. Representative Ruth Thompson of Michigan. She proposed legislation (not passed), banning the mailing or transport of any "obscene, lewd, lascivious or filthy [disc] or other article capable of producing sound."[17] This was a clear attempt to restrict or arrest the spread of rhythm and blues singles, which were growing in popularity.

Rock 'n' roll and now rap exemplify the anxiety present in the commercialization of minority voices, in the conflict between the money to be made in a free market and the lack of control over cultural production. Associated with youth, rock 'n' roll has always been viewed by the purists as an oppositional voice. Unlike pop, it does not conform into a safe, neat, commercial package. The threatening nature of rock music has always made it commercially successful. As Ice-T points out, "If you bounce along and sing about milk shakes and homework, you're doing popular music, but if you rock that fuckin' system, you're doing rock 'n' roll, regardless of what instruments you use. My key with *Body Count* is to talk about things that are interesting to the black community *and* the white community."[18]

The scrutiny of rap music by the Parents' Music Resource Center (PRMC) may partially account for Ice-T's foray into hardcore rock with *Body Count*. But given the commercial interests, the attempts at regulation of content as a form of social control seem relatively futile. What is curious about the controversy surrounding "Cop Killer" is that it took so long to erupt. The song debuted in the summer of 1991 on the Lollapalooza tour, was recorded in the fall, and was released in March 1992. The controversy didn't erupt until June 1992. Figuratively, "Cop Killer" is about fighting back and getting even, about taking charge and not just resisting. The timing of the controversy surrounding it suggests a reaction to another event covered nationally in the last week of April: the Los Angeles riots.

The exhaustive coverage of the Los Angeles riots in late April was a counterpart to the repeated showings of the videotape of the Rodney King beating. The two form a text (Rodney King) and countertext (Los Angeles riots) of images, first being contained and subdued and then fighting back in retribution. To the viewing audience, some spectacular reversals occurred; an instrument of criminal surveillance was used on the police, and the jury acquitting the officers seemed to deny the validity of the drama repeatedly played out on the nightly news. When the riots erupted and continued over several days, previous boundaries and their meanings were further confused. The Los Angeles police were absent and ineffective. The validity of these symbols of authority was seriously called into question, this time to mainstream viewers through the documentary status of news footage. As one journalist noted, "Blacks were not the only ones burning down the buildings. This rebellion was a true picture of the 'Rainbow' coalition. Whites, Blacks, Mexicans, Hispanics, Asians, Samoans, Arabs—people from all walks of life sent a message to the elite of America."[19] If the message of the riots was confused and debatable, the question raised by the nightly drama of angry masses taking control was clear and simple: "Who's in charge here?"

"Cop Killer" is a fantasy of getting even. It depicts a member of an outgroup taking extreme action. It is the last angry cut on an album written in response to injustice, police brutality, and the denial of legitimate recourse to those populating the margins. That it is hateful, vengeful, and threatening is undeniable; however, it does not organize opposition as much as it dramatizes the state of mind of the powerless. It is an excoriating expression of black rage that deliberately offers no solutions. "Cop

Killer" works within a tradition of black music's use of hyperbole and conforms to the type of speech described by Frederick Douglass when he related the role of his speech to social conditions of blacks. "At a time like this, scorching irony, not convincing argument is needed. Oh, had I the ability and could I reach the nation's ear, I would pour out a stream of biting ridicule, blasting reproach, withering sarcasm, and stern rebuke. For it is not light that is needed but fire; it is not the gentle shower but thunder."[20]

Ice-T has defended *Body Count* as an editorial and invoked the First Amendment. Yet a coalition of state officials has successfully restricted Ice-T's free speech by exerting public pressure on commercial outlets through a massive campaign—a case of state actors interfering with private speech.[21] Time-Warner has removed the offending track from *Body Count* and reissued it. Moreover, other rap artists on labels owned by Time-Warner have been asked "to alter or remove cop-related tracks from their forthcoming releases."[22] Underlying the juxtaposition of the Los Angeles riots and the Ice-T boycott is the narrative that "Cop Killer" incited the masses to action; the song, not the Rodney King verdict and the police brutality that was on trial, caused the riots. Thus, a narrative has been constructed that reassigns blame; a demagogue incites the volatile and irrational masses to insurrection. Silence the voice and you have removed the problem.

The media images of the Los Angeles riots presented an opportunity for authority to mobilize against the voices of the inner-city represented by the rappers. As rapper Chuck D has often been quoted as saying, "rap is the CNN of Black America." By linking disorder with rap music and its incumbent associations, the coalition of police and legislators appropriated a convincing soundtrack for the images dispersed through television. The pressure placed on commercial outlets has effectively restricted the flow and the content of rap music, yet Ice-T starred with rapper Ice Cube in the movie *Trespass*. And his album, *Home Invasion*, threatened further violation of previous cultural boundaries. The media itself, then, becomes an area of territorial conflict; hence, the battle is to decide who and what may appear or be heard there. Symbolic politics, issues of control and silence and exclusion, are evident in the formation of groups for improvement or protection—such as The Coalition for Better Television—and explain the logic of shutting down dialogue in mass culture. It is an attempt to restore traditional social arrangements and reduce diversity.

Images of chaos circulated in the media and associated with rappers and black urban youth reinforce conservative arguments for control but not for real reform. The immediate recourse of the Bush-Reagan administration in assigning blame for the Los Angeles riots to the relaxed liberal policies of the 1960s seeks to remove the problem from the realm of action to the realm of the symbolic. In doing so, they conform to a reactionary model characteristic of political extremism. "In almost every generation," Lipset and Raab write in their study on political extremism, "old American groups which saw themselves displaced, relatively demoted in status and power by processes rooted in social change, have sought to reverse these processes through the processes of moralistic movements or political action groups."[23] That this will be increasingly difficult to do and that mass culture will be the site of many more battles has less to do with social enlightenment than with the exigencies of the market. Rap music is a viable commercial force, becoming increasingly mainstream. (Time-Warner even embarked on publishing the *VIBE*, a magazine that positions itself as the *Rolling Stone* of hip-hop culture.) Whether commercial success will compromise rap even more than citizens' action groups remains to be seen. One explanation for the resistance to rap is that it is a subculture transmitted to a mainstream still learning to read it; this accounts for the controversy, the misreadings, the confusion of cultural codes. Certainly the message of rap, as of any subculture, is the demand not only to be heard but to be listened to. As Dick Hebdige points out in his study of subculture:

The "subcultural response" is neither simply affirmation nor refusal, neither "commercial exploitation" nor a "genuine revolt." It is neither simply resistance against some external order nor straightforward conformity with the parent culture. It is both a declaration of independence, of otherness, of alien intent, a refusal of anonymity, of subordinate status. It is an insubordination. And at the same time it is also a confirmation of the fact of the powerlessness, a celebration of impotence. Subcultures are both a play for attention and a refusal, once attention has been granted, to be read according to the Book.[24]

This oppositional stance was confirmed by Ice-T's remarks that:

The people in the [heavy] metal community, the people in my posse, we all have to connect with our allies, consolidate, create one big posse. The key in America is to keep us separate, hating each other, fighting. Once we really find out who's on our side, we'll gain a lot of power. That's the first thing we're trying to do right now with the music; trying to organize all the people who want to really go and fight and get things together. That's stage one."[25]

The "Cop Killer" controversy notwithstanding, the culture wars in the battlefield of mass culture have barely begun.

NOTES

1. Matthew Arnold, *Culture and Anarchy* (New Haven, CT: Yale University Press, 1994).
2. Richard Bolton, ed., *Culture Wars* (New York: The New Press, 1992), p. 337.
3. Bolton, *op. cit*, p. 4.
4. Pat Buchanan, "Losing the War for America's Culture?" *Washington Times*, May 22, 1989.
5. Ibid.
6. Bolton, *op. cit.*, p. 332.
7. Hilton Kramer, "Is Art Above the Laws of Decency," *New York Times*, July 2, 1989.
8. Ibid.
9. Pat Buchanan, *op. cit.*
10. Carol S. Vance, "The War on Culture," *Art in America*, Sept. 1989.
11. Clement Greenberg, *Dallas Observer*, October 8, 1992.
12. Greenberg, *op. cit.*
13. Brian Wallis, *Art After Modernism: Rethinking Representation* (New York: The New Museum of Contemporary Art, 1984), p. xi.
14. Wallis, *op. cit.*, p. xiii.
15. Bolton, *op. cit.*

16. Ice-T (reprint of 1992 interview) by Alan Light in *Rolling Stone*, Oct. 15, 1992, n. 641, p. 162 (2).

17. Anthony DeCurtis, "Ice-T Song 'Cop-Killer' Causes Controversy," *Rolling Stone*, Sept. 17, 1992, n. 639, p. 32 (1).

18. Ice-T, Holly George-Warren, *OPTION*, March/April 1992 [Clipfile].

19. Ice-T, Holly George-Warren, *OPTION*, March/April 1992 [Clipfile].

20. Frederick Douglass, *Narrative of the Life of Frederick Douglass, an American Slave*, Cambridge, MA, Belkamp Press, 1960, xxvi, 163 pages.

21. Alan Light, "Rap. (Political Candidates and Police Target Rap Music as a Bad Influence) (1992 Yearbook)," *Rolling Stone*, Dec. 10, 1992, nn. 645–646, p. 79(1).

22. Kim Neely, "'Cop-Killer' Aftershocks," *Rolling Stone*, Oct. 29, 1992, n. 642, p. 32(1).

23. Seymour Martin Lipset & Earl Raab, *The Politics of Unreason: Right-Wing Extremism in America, 1790-1970* (New York: Harper & Row, 1970), p. xvii.

24. Dick Hebdige, *Subculture: The Meaning of Style* (London: Methuen & Co. Ltd., 1979), p. 35.

25. Ice-T, Holly George-Warren, *OPTION*, March/April 1992 [Clipfile].

APPENDIX: THE NATIONAL ENDOWMENT FOR THE ARTS

To promote the arts, Congress created the National Endowment for the Arts (NEA) in 1965.

In the late 1980s, part of the NEA's funds were used to support Robert Mapplethorpe's homoerotic photographs. On October 5, 1990, a jury acquitted Cincinnati's Contemporary Arts Center and its director, Dennis Barrie, of misdemeanor charges of pandering obscenity and illegal use of a minor in nudity-oriented materials. A grand jury had indicted the Center and its director over its exhibit of 175 photographs entitled "Robert Mapplethorpe: The Perfect Moment."

Part of NEA's funds supported Andres Serrano's "Piss Christ," a photograph of a crucifix inside a container of urine. Not surprisingly, complaints ensued and Senator Jesse Helms led a legislative charge against such use of public funds. Following are selected statutes concerning the NEA and portions of a 1998 Supreme Court decision that upholds § 954(d)(1) of the NEA statutes. In that statutory provision, Congress directs the NEA to take into consideration "general standards of decency and respect" when judging grant applications.

NATIONAL FOUNDATION ON THE ARTS AND THE HUMANITIES

Title 20 United States Code

§ 952. Definitions

As used in this Act—

(j) The term "determined to be obscene" means determined, in a final judgment of a court of record and of competent jurisdiction in the United States, to be obscene.

(l) The term "obscene" means with respect to a project, production, workshop, or program that—

(1) the average person, applying contemporary community standards, would find that such project, production, workshop, or program, when taken as a whole, appeals to the prurient interest;

(2) such project, production, workshop, or program depicts or describes sexual conduct in a patently offensive way; and

(3) such project, production, workshop, or program, when taken as a whole, lacks serious literary, artistic, political, or scientific value.

§ 954. National Endowment for the Arts

(a) Establishment.   There is established within the Foundation a National Endowment for the Arts.

. . .

(c) Program of contracts, grants-in-aid, or loans to groups and individuals for projects and productions; traditionally underrepresented recipients of financial assistance. The Chairperson, with the advice of the National Council on the Arts, is authorized to establish and carry out a program of contracts with, or grants-in-aid or loans to, groups or, in appropriate cases, individuals of exceptional talent engaged in or concerned with the arts.

(d) Application for payment; regulations and procedures. No payment shall be made under this section except upon application therefor which is submitted to the National Endowment for the Arts in accordance with regulations issued and procedures established by the Chairperson. In establishing such regulations and procedures, the Chairperson shall ensure that—

(1) artistic excellence and artistic merit are the criteria by which applications are judged, taking into consideration general standards of decency and respect for the diverse beliefs and values of the American public; and

(2) applications are consistent with the purpose of this section. Such regulations and procedures shall clearly indicate that obscenity is without artistic merit, is not protected speech, and shall not be funded. Projects, productions, workshops, and programs that are determined to be obscene are prohibited from receiving financial assistance under this Act from the National Endowment for the Arts.

The disapproval or approval of an application by the Chairperson shall not be construed to mean, and shall not be considered as evidence that, the project, production, workshop, or program for which the applicant requested financial assistance is or is not obscene.

. . .

(k) Reviews to ensure compliance with regulations. The Inspector General of the Endowment shall conduct appropriate reviews to ensure that recipients of financial assistance under this section comply with the regulations under this Act that apply with respect to such assistance, including regulations relating to accounting and financial matters.

(l) Use of financial assistance for obscene project, production, etc.; repayment of assistance; exceptions.

(1) If, after reasonable notice and opportunity for a hearing on the record, the Chairperson determines that a recipient of financial assistance provided under this section by the Chairperson or any non-Federal entity, used such financial assistance for a project, production, workshop, or program that is determined to be obscene, then the Chairperson shall require that until such recipient repays such assistance (in such amount, and under such terms and conditions, as the Chairperson determines to be appropriate) to the Endowment; no subsequent financial assistance to be provided under this section to such recipient. . . .

[An October 23, 1989 Amendment established a commission to review actions of the NEA, but the legislation also provided that the commission would cease functioning on September 30, 1990. Excerpts of the text of this Amendment, included under notes to 20 U.S.C. § 954, follows below.]

Prohibition against use of funds for obscene materials; creation of Independent Commission to review grant-making procedures. Act Oct. 23, 1989, P.L. 101-121, Title III, § 304(a)-(c), 103 Stat. 741, provides:

"(a) None of the funds authorized to be appropriated for the National Endowment for the Arts or the National Endowment for the Humanities may be used to promote, disseminate, or produce materials which in the judgment of the National Endowment for the Arts or the National Endowment for the Humanities may be considered obscene, including but not limited to, depictions of sadomasochism, homoeroticism, the sexual exploitation of children, or individuals engaged in sex acts and which, when taken as a whole, do not have serious literary, artistic, political, or scientific value.

"(b) It is the sense of the Congress:

"(1) That under the present procedures employed for awarding National Endowment for the Arts grants, although the National Endowment for the Arts has had an excellent record over the years, it is possible for projects to be funded without adequate review of the artistic content or value of the work.

"(2) That recently works have been funded which are without artistic value but which are criticized as pornographic and shocking by any standards.

"(3) That censorship inhibits and stultifies the full expression of art.

"(4) That free inquiry and expression is reaffirmed. Therefore, be it resolved:

"(A) That all artistic works do not have artistic or humanistic excellence and an application can include works that possess both nonexcellent and excellent portions.

"(B) That the Chairman of the National Endowment for the arts has the responsibility to determine whether such an application should be funded.

"(C) That the National Endowment for the Arts must find a better method to seek out those works that have artistic excellence and to exclude those works which are without any redeeming literary, scholarly, cultural, or artistic value.

"(D) That a commission be established to review the National Endowment for the Arts grant making procedures, including those of its panel system, to determine whether there should be standards for grant making other than 'substantial artistic and cultural significance, giving emphasis to American creativity and cultural diversity and the maintenance and encouragement of professional excellence' (20 U.S.C. 954(c)(1)) and if so, then what other standards. The criteria to be considered by the commission shall include but not be limited to possible standards where (a) applying contemporary community standards would find that the work taken as a whole appeals to a prurient interest; (b) the work depicts or describes in a patently offensive way, sexual conduct; and (c) the work, taken as a whole, lacks serious artistic and cultural value."

NATIONAL ENDOWMENT FOR THE ARTS v. FINLEY
SUPREME COURT OF THE UNITED STATES

March 31, 1998, Argued
June 25, 1998, Decided

DISPOSITION: 100 F.3d 671, reversed and remanded.

[Justice O'Connor delivered the 8-to-1 opinion of the Court. Justice Souter filed a dissenting opinion.]

SYLLABUS: The National Foundation on the Arts and Humanities Act vests the National Endowment for the Arts (NEA) with substantial discretion to award financial grants to support the arts; it identifies only the broadest funding priorities, including "artistic and cultural significance, giving emphasis to . . . creativity and cultural diversity," "professional excellence," and the encouragement of "public . . . education . . . and appreciation of the arts." See 20 U.S.C. § 954(c)(1)-(10). Applications for NEA funding are initially reviewed by advisory panels of experts in the relevant artistic field. The panels report to the National Council on the Arts (Council), which, in turn, advises the NEA Chairperson. In 1989, controversial photographs that appeared in two NEA-funded exhibits prompted public outcry over the agency's grant-making procedures. Congress reacted to the controversy by inserting an amendment into the NEA's 1990 reauthorization bill. The amendment became § 954(d)(1), which directs the Chairperson to ensure that "artistic excellence and artistic merit are the criteria by which [grant] applications are judged, taking into consideration general standards of decency and respect for the diverse beliefs and values of the American public." The NEA has not promulgated an official interpretation of the provision, but the Council adopted a resolution to implement § 954(d)(1) by ensuring that advisory panel members represent geographic, ethnic, and aesthetic diversity. The four individual respondents are performance artists who applied for NEA grants before § 954(d)(1) was enacted. An advisory panel recommended approval of each of their projects, but the Council subsequently recommended disapproval, and funding was denied. They filed sq)u for restoration of the recommended grants or reconsideration of their applications, asserting First Amendment and statutory claims. When Congress enacted § 954(d)(1), respondents, joined by the National Association of Artists' Organizations, amended their complaint to challenge the provision as void for vagueness and impermissibly viewpoint based. The District Court granted summary judgment in favor of respondents on their facial constitutional challenge to § 954(d)(1). The Ninth Circuit affirmed, holding that § 954(d)(1), on its face, impermissibly discriminates on the basis of viewpoint and is void for vagueness under the First and Fifth Amendments.

Held: Section 954(d)(1) is facially valid, as it neither inherently interferes with First Amendment rights nor violates constitutional vagueness principles.

(a) Respondents confront a heavy burden in advancing their facial constitutional challenge, and they have not demonstrated a substantial risk that application of § 954(d)(1) will lead to the suppression of free expression. . . . The premise of respondents' claim is that § 954(d)(1) constrains the agency's ability to fund certain categories of artistic expression. The provision, however, simply adds "considerations" to the grant-making process; it does not preclude awards to projects that might be deemed "indecent" or "disrespectful," nor place conditions on grants, or even specify that those factors must be given any particular weight in reviewing an application. Regardless whether the NEA's view that the formulation of diverse advisory panels is sufficient to comply with Congress' command is in fact a reasonable reading, § 954(d)(1)'s plain text clearly does not impose a categorical requirement. Furthermore, the political context surrounding the "decency and respect" clause's adoption is inconsistent with respondents' assertion. The legislation was a bipartisan proposal introduced as a counterweight to amendments that would have eliminated the NEA's funding or substantially constrained its grant-making authority. Section 954(d)(1) merely admonishes the NEA to take "decency and respect" into consideration, and the Court does not perceive a realistic danger that it will be utilized to preclude or punish the expression of particular views. The Court typically strikes down legislation as facially unconstitutional when the dangers are both more evident and more substantial. . . . Given the varied interpretations of the "decency and respect" criteria urged by the parties, and the provision's vague exhortation to "take them into consideration," it seems unlikely that § 954(d)(1) will significantly compromise First Amendment values.

The NEA's enabling statute contemplates a number of indisputably constitutional applications for both the "decency" and the "respect" prong of § 954(d)(1). It is well established that "decency" is a permissible factor where "educational suitability" motivates its consideration. . . . And the statute already provides that the agency must take "cultural diversity" into account. References to permissible applications would

not alone be sufficient to sustain the statute, but neither is the Court persuaded that, in other applications, the language of § 954(d)(1) itself will give rise to the suppression of protected expression. Any content-based considerations that may be taken into account are a consequence of the nature of arts funding; the NEA has limited resources to allocate among many "artistically excellent" projects, and it does so on the basis of a wide variety of subjective criteria. . . . Moreover, although the First Amendment applies in the subsidy context, Congress has wide latitude to set spending priorities. . . . Unless and until § 954(d)(1) is applied in a manner that raises concern about the suppression of disfavored viewpoints, the Court will uphold it. . . .

(b) The lower courts also erred in invalidating § 954(d)(1) as unconstitutionally vague. The First and Fifth Amendments protect speakers from arbitrary and discriminatory enforcement of vague standards. . . . Section 954(d)(1)'s terms are undeniably opaque, and if they appeared in a criminal statute or regulatory scheme, they could raise substantial vagueness concerns. It is unlikely, however, that speakers will be compelled to steer too far clear of any forbidden area in the context of NEA grants. As a practical matter, artists may conform their speech to what they believe to be the NEA decision making criteria in order to acquire funding. But when the Government is acting as patron rather than sovereign, the consequences of imprecision are not constitutionally severe. In the context of selective subsidies, it is not always feasible for Congress to legislate with clarity. Indeed, to accept respondents' vagueness argument would be to call into question the constitutionality of the many valuable Government programs awarding scholarships and grants on the basis of subjective criteria such as "excellence." . . .

Justice Souter, dissenting:

. . .

The decency and respect proviso mandates viewpoint-based decisions in the disbursement of government subsidies, and the Government has wholly failed to explain why the statute should be afforded an exemption from the fundamental rule of the First Amendment that viewpoint discrimination in the exercise of public authority over expressive activity is unconstitutional. The Court's conclusions that the proviso is not viewpoint based, that it is not a regulation, and that the NEA may permissibly engage in viewpoint-based discrimination, are all patently mistaken. . . .

5

Stern Stuff: Here Comes the FCC

Sandra Davidson

> "[I]t is . . . often true that one man's vulgarity is another's lyric."
>
> —*Cohen v. California*, 403 U.S. 15, 25 (1971).

The Federal Communications Commission (FCC) polices broadcast airwaves—with the help of the public. Instead of monitoring the airwaves, the FCC responds to complaints by listeners. Then the FCC can haul out a heavy arsenal of weapons against what it considers broadcast indecency. Often the result is steep fines against broadcasters for raunchy words—whether spoken or sung.

According to the FCC's current definition, "indecency" is "[l]anguage or material that, in context, depicts or describes, in terms patently offensive as measured by contemporary community standards for the broadcast medium, sexual or excretory activities of organs."[1]

The definition of "indecency" is vague; the fines, however, are not. They're spelled out in dollar signs and numerals. The undisputed king of FCC fines is Howard Stern, with a total of $1.7 million in fines against Infinity Broadcasting Corporation. Stern keeps falling over the "indecency" line drawn by the FCC.[2] Of course, the FCC has lots of help, such as volunteer Al Westcott, who has monitored Stern's broadcasts and mailed transcripts of them to the FCC. Westcott's concern, he says, is "latchkey children, who do not have parents at home to tell them that the behavior Howard Stern is advocating is inappropriate."[3]

"America's No. 1 'Shock Jock,'"[4] Stern both entertains and offends, from his Lesbian Dial-A-Date contest[5] to his Musical Crotches game. FCC Commissioner James Quello commented, "I find Howard Stern to be a rather entertaining smart ass."[6] Of course, the comment appeared in print; Quello surely would not want the word "ass" to be broadcast. As for Stern's crudeness, a commentator says, "Mr. Stern did not invent the adolescent male's disgusted [*sic*] fascination with genitalia and bodily fluids; he only capitalizes on it."[7] But such capitalizing comes at an expense.

When Stern or disk jockeys who like ribald lyrics fall over the line, they drag with them the radio stations that carry their shows. The stations get to pick up the tab, and doing business is becoming more and more expensive for broadcasters.

A BRIEF HISTORY OF INDECENCY LAW

All the squabbling over indecency started in October 1973 when a New York radio station aired George Carlin's monologue "Filthy Words," detailing the seven filthy words that Carlin said could not be used over the airwaves. The 12-minute monologue aired at 2:00 on a Tuesday afternoon. A father who heard it with his son was not amused and complained to the FCC.[8]

In *FCC v. Pacifica*, the U.S. Supreme Court ruled five to four that the FCC could forbid broadcasting of the "seven filthy words" during times when children might be listening to the radio. The words, though "indecent," were "not obscene."[9] But Congress had declared that radio broadcasting of "any obscene, indecent, *or* profane language" was a crime.[10] Use of the disjunctive "or" meant that being indecent was enough for a broadcaster to be in trouble. "Prurient appeal," a necessary element in obscenity, was not necessary for words to be indecent, according to the Court.[11] The case dashed broadcasters' hopes that the Supreme Court would give them the same amount of constitutional protection that the Court gives print media. The Court said:

We have long recognized that each medium of expression presents special First Amendment problems. . . . And of all forms of communication, it is broadcasting that has received the most limited First Amendment protection.

The reasons for these distinctions are complex, but two have relevance to the present case. First, the broadcast media have established a uniquely pervasive presence in the lives of all Americans. Patently offensive, indecent material presented over the airwaves confronts the citizen, not only in public, but also in the privacy of the home, where the individual's right to be left alone plainly outweighs the First Amendment rights of an intruder. . . . Because the broadcast audience is constantly tuning in and out, prior warnings cannot completely protect the listener or viewer from unexpected program content. To say that one may avoid further offense by turning off the radio when he [or she] hears indecent language is like saying that the remedy for an assault is to run away after the first blow.

Second, broadcasting is uniquely accessible to children, even those too young to read. . . . Pacifica's broadcast could have enlarged a child's vocabulary in an instant.[12]

Until 1987, however, the FCC took a narrow view of what it considered "indecent." So long as broadcasts did not contain Carlin's "seven filthy words," the FCC left the broadcasters alone.[13] But then the FCC concluded that "the highly restrictive enforcement standard employed after the . . . *Pacifica* decision was unduly narrow as a matter of law."[14]

And, until 1987, the FCC had taken no action against indecency broadcast after 10:00 PM.[15]   But the FCC changed its view on that, as well.   Citing "available evidence" that "suggested there were still significant numbers of children" listening to radio after 10:00 PM, the FCC warned broadcasters that they "should no longer assume" that broadcasting indecency after 10:00 PM. would be "automatically" safe. Instead, the FCC said, it would consider indecency actionable "if broadcast when there is a reasonable risk that children may be in the audience, a determination that was to be based on ratings data on a market-by-market basis."[16]

On April 16, 1987, the FCC announced its new guidelines.[17] It did so in trying to clarify for three broadcast stations the formal warning letters they had received—Infinity Broadcasting Corporation of Pennsylvania, WYSP-FM, for the morning drive-time Howard Stern show; the University of California-Santa Barbara, KCSB-FM, for late-night airing of the song "Makin' Bacon" by the Pork Dukes; and Pacification Foundation, Inc., of Los Angeles, KPFK-FM, for airing after 10:00 PM a play about homosexuals, *The Jerker*.[18]

Note that in stepping up its attempts to keep "blue" radio from the tender ears of children in 1987, the FCC was attempting to fine two radio stations for indecency aired after 10:00 PM—a time that fell into the former 10:00 PM to 6:00 AM "safe harbor."[19]   Morality in Media (MIM), a New York-based anti-pornography organization,[20] had been in the thick of the controversy, arguing that there should be no safe harbor whatsoever because the statutory prohibition against indecency was "absolute and unqualified."[21]   On first hearing of the FCC's plans to take stepped-up action against broadcast indecency, MIM hailed the FCC's movement as a "refreshing shower after eight years in a desert of overheated rock lyrics and scatological disc jockeys."[22]

But in the first of a series of suits called *Action for Children's Television v. FCC* (a case commonly referred to as *Act I*), the federal Circuit Court of Appeals for the District of Columbia turned the shower cold by bringing the FCC up short. Although the court upheld the warning for the Howard Stern show, the court vacated the warnings for the post-10:00 PM broadcasts and declared that the FCC had to have a "reasonable safe harbor rule."[23] The court ordered the FCC to determine at what times indecency could be safely aired.[24] This decision was written by Judge Ruth Bader Ginsburg, the second woman to become a Supreme Court Justice.

Although legal writing style calls for listing only the first plaintiff and the first defendant in the name of a case, the list of suers in the *Action for Children's Television v. FCC* cases was long. Joining the group Action for Children's Television were: American Civil Liberties Union, The Association of Independent Television Stations, Inc., Capital Cities/ABC, Inc., CBS, Inc., Fox Television Stations, Inc., Greater Media, Inc., Infinity Broadcasting Corporation (the corporation that ended up with $1.7 million in fines for broadcasting Howard Stern programs), Motion Picture Association of America, Inc., National Association of Broadcasters, National Public Radio, People for the American Way, Post-Newsweek Stations, Inc., Public Broadcasting Service, Radio-Television News Directors Association, Reporters Committee for Freedom of the Press, and the Society of Professional Journalists. Joining together in another suit that the court consolidated into a single suit were:

Pacifica Foundation, National Federation of Community Broadcasters, American Public Radio, National Association of College Broadcasters, Intercollegiate Broadcast System, Pen American Center, and Allen Ginsberg.

The defendants in the suit were the FCC and the United States of America. Siding with the defendants as "friends of the court" (amici curiae) were Morality in Media, National Family Legal Foundation, American Family Association, Focus on the Family, National Law Center for Children and Families, Concerned Women of America, National Coalition Against Pornography, National Association of Evangelicals, Religious Alliance Against Pornography, Family Research Council, and the National Religious Broadcasters.

But after Judge Ginsburg's decision supporting a "safe harbor" for indecency, Congress jumped into the fray and declared a 24-hour indecency ban in an appropriations rider.[25] Senator Jesse Helms sponsored the law.[26] The FCC then answered a suit to stay enforcement of the 24-hour ban with its findings, made after soliciting public comments, of a "reasonable risk that significant numbers of children ages 17 and under listen to radio and view television at all times" without parental supervision. Thus, the government's compelling interest in protecting these children necessitated a 24-hour ban; no less restrictive alternative existed, the FCC argued.[27]

But in 1991, the U.S. Circuit Court of Appeals for the District of Columbia, in *Act II*, struck down the 24-hour ban on First Amendment grounds. A 24-hour ban simply was not narrowly enough tailored. It was too restrictive, the court decided.[28] The FCC was caught between Congress and a determined court. The court said:

We appreciate the Commission's constraints in responding to the appropriations rider. It would be unseemly for a regulatory agency to throw down the gauntlet, even a gauntlet grounded on the Constitution, to Congress. But just as the FCC may not ignore the dictates of the legislative branch, neither may the judiciary ignore its independent duty to check the constitutional excesses of Congress. We hold that Congress' action here cannot preclude the Commission from creating a safe harbor exception to its regulation of indecent broadcasts.[29]

Bowing to the court's power, the Senate, by a vote of 93 to 3,[30] passed a bill creating a 10 PM until 6 AM safe harbor for public (noncommercial) radio stations and for all stations that do not air past midnight, and a six-hour safe harbor for indecency—midnight until 6:00 AM—for all other stations. President Bush signed the law on August 26, 1992.[31]

Another attack in the U.S. Court of Appeals for the District of Columbia, *Act III*, tested these limited hours for "indecency."[32] But on February 16, 1994, the Court of Appeals vacated its November order and decided to rehear the safe harbor case.[33] In June 1995, in *Act IV*, the court upheld "channeling" of indecent broadcasts between 10:00 PM and 6:00 AM to protect children under 18.[34] The following month, in *Act V*, the court approved the FCC's producers, approving the dismissal of the constitutional challenges to the FCC's "scheme for imposing forfeitures for the broadcast of indecent material."[35]

The net result of the court's decisions is that the FCC can continue its crack-down on indecency, but it must tolerate indecency one-third of the time, during the 10:00 PM to 6:00 AM safe harbor.

Another important historical fact is this: In 1989, Congress multiplied over tenfold the maximum fine the FCC could levy—*from $20,000 to $250,000.*[36]

In short, there is a safe harbor for indecency, but the fines can be huge for violations that occur outside of those safe-harbor hours. Unfortunately, the safe-harbor hours are not the lucrative drive-time hours that Howard Stern's show occupies. Nor are the safe-harbor hours prime time for many who like their rap or rock a little "raw."

LYRICS THE FCC SCORNED

Music, of course, sends messages, and sometimes the FCC disapproves lyrical language. Music, more or less, first got Stern into trouble with the FCC. The year was 1988—the year after the FCC turned up the heat on indecency—and the fine was $6,000 for Infinity Broadcasting Corporation. Three of its stations had broadcast Stern's piece, which included a man playing the piano, but not with his hands.[37]

1989 was a busy year for the FCC, as it worked to clear a backlog of indecency cases that had been piling up since 1987.[38] Many FCC fines have been for lyrics that are on the "bawdy" side. For example, the FCC let a University of California station, KCSB-FM in Santa Barbara, out of the frying pan for playing "Makin' Bacon" by the Pork Dukes. The station, did, however, receive a warning.[39] Not so lucky was Las Vegas station KLUC-FM, which received a $2,000 fine in 1989 for playing Prince's "Erotic City."[40]

In 1989, Miami station WZTA-FM, received a $2,000 fine for playing the song "Penis Envy," which it aired in 1987.[41] Likewise, WLLZ-FM in Detroit took a $2,000 loss the same year for "Walk With an Erection."[42] The song uses the tune to "Walk Like an Egyptian." WIOD-AM in Miami received a $10,000 fine, $2,000 apiece for a "Butch Beer Commercial," which includes singing, and for four songs—"Penis Envy," "Walk with an Erection," "Jet Boy, Jet Girl," and "Candy Wrapper."[43] In late 1989, Evergreen Broadcasting received a $6,000 fine for broadcasts on Chicago station WLUP-AM in 1987 and 1989.[44] One broadcast included a telephone caller's singing of the song "Kiddie Porn."[45] And, the Charlotte, Michigan station WMMQ-FM narrowly missed an indecency fine for its 1989 broadcast of a song about pubic hair.[46]

In 1990, WFBQ-FM Indianapolis, owned by Greater American Broadcasting, got slapped with a $10,000 fine for airing indecency in 1987 over the "Bob and Tom Show."[47] Among other things, Bob and Tom aired "Butch Beer," "Candy Wrapper," and "Stroke Your Dingy."[48] Also, for 1990 airings of the songs "Candy Wrapper" and "Sit on My Face," KGB-FM in San Diego took a $25,000 hit from the FCC.[49] "Sit on My Face" is a Monty Python song.[50] College station WSUC-FM in Cortland, New York, received a fine for playing a "vulgar" rap song.[51]

In 1992, the FCC sent Evergreen a new letter of inquiry for, among other things, broadcasting over WLUP-Chicago the song "Venus" with new lyrics.[52] Los Angeles station KLSX-FM received the heaviest FCC fine up to that date in October 1992—$105,000 for airing Stern. The fine was based on approximately 30 minutes worth of material culled from over 50 hours of broadcasting done between October 30 and December 6, 1991.[53] It was Al Westcott who filed the 47-page complaint.[54] The hit came about, in part, because of Stern's broadcast of the "Magic Johnson Song," sung by Howard Stern himself on November 15, 1991.

The American Civil Liberties Union (ACLU) came to Stern's defense, filing a 22-page brief with the FCC to argue, among other things, that the popularity of the show (it was Number 1 in New York, Los Angeles, and Philadelphia) demonstrates that it is not offensive by community standards;[55] that the commission's rulings on indecency are so contradictory that its "indecency standard" is "unconstitutionally vague";[56] and that no data show that children listen to Stern. Even if they did, the ACLU argued,

[T]he pertinent psychological research demonstrates that children would not understand most of the allegedly indecent material broadcast on the show and that the scant matter of that nature that they might understand—the "bathroom" or "scatological" humor in which Stern occasionally engages—would not harm them because it is similar to the jokes they hear and tell on the playground.[57]

The day after the fine came down, Stern's program featured Butt Bongo.[58] The "latest craze" on his show, Butt Bongo is performed to music by male Stern fans who bongo on their female partners' bare bottoms.[59]

Less than two months later, on December 18, 1992, the five FCC commissioners voted unanimously to fine Infinity Broadcasting Corporation $600,000 for airing Stern's morning show on three stations in New York over WXRK-FM, Philadelphia over WYSP-FM, and Washington, D.C., over WJFK-FM.[60] The $200,000 fines on each station came about, in part, because of their broadcasting of the "Magic Johnson Song" on November 15, 1991, simultaneously with Los Angeles station KLSX-FM, which received the earlier fine of $105,000.[61]

Infinity's official response to the fine was "based on two principles," Infinity's attorney said. "One, does the material in question fall within the indecency definition? And two, given the absence of children listening to the 'Howard Stern Show,' is there compelling reason for governmental intercession?"[62]

On the same day as the unanimous vote on the fines, by a four-to-one vote, the FCC also decided to let Infinity purchase three radio licenses. Then-Chairman Al Sikes dissented.[63] In dissenting to the purchase of the three Cook Inlet stations,[64] Sikes said, "Perhaps Infinity's management has viewed our indecency fines merely as a cost of doing business." And Sikes called the complaint that KLSX in Los Angeles had aired indecency from the Stern show on November 9 through 15—after the station had received its $105,000 fine—the "proverbial straw that breaks the camel's back."[65] Clearly hoping to get Infinity's attention, the FCC also warned that if Infinity received any further indecency violations, the FCC may initiate license revocation proceedings.[66]

In August 1993, the FCC fined a non-Infinity station, KFBI in Las Vegas, $74,000 for airing Stern, and the FCC fined Infinity another $500,000.[67] In February 1994,

Infinity received a $400,000 fine for airing Stern.[68] The total in fines for Infinity is nearly $1.7 million.

The FCC also handed out smaller fines. In 1994, the FCC imposed a $12,500 fine on a Dallas station, KNON-FM, for a 1992 broadcast of the song "I Want to Be a Homosexual."[69] In 1996, the FCC handed down another fine for Prince's song "Erotic City"—$7,500 to San Antonio station KTFM-FM.[70] These fines, of course, paled in comparison to Infinity's fines.

Infinity implemented a seven-second delay and is monitoring Stern's programs. In October 1994, FCC Commissioner James Quello told attendees of a conference in Washington, D.C., sponsored by *Broadcasting & Cable* magazine: "We're now in the process of figuring out what to do with that $1.7 million fine. I've had the opportunity to listen to Stern recently, and they've made a definite effort to cut down on indecency. Some of the stuff is raunchy, but it does not go over the border."[71]

These fines for indecency are Stern stuff! What can radio stations that want to air conversations and lyrics that are not "PG-13" do? Just settle for the "play and pay" game? Fines can amount to steep overhead, even given how well "blue" humor sells.

In 1992, Infinity decided not to pay any of its fines.[72] At least one other radio company fought its fine. Evergreen Broadcasting, which owns Chicago station WLUP, refused to pay its $6,000 fine for broadcasts in 1987 and 1989. (The fine resulted, in part, from a telephone caller's singing of the song "Kiddie Porn.")[73] The decision to fight was a matter of principle, not principal,[74] because fighting a fine costs many thousands of dollars more in attorney's fees than simply paying a fine would cost. Evergreen was the first broadcast company to refuse to pay a fine.

Refusing to pay is the only alternative to paying because the Communications Act does not provide for appealing fines.[75] In informing the FCC that it would not pay, Evergreen explained that it "sincerely believes that the Commission's policies on broadcast indecency are unconstitutionally vague and unworkable and that they can and do have a chilling effect."[76] The Justice Department filed suit in the federal district court in Chicago against Evergreen.[77] But to collect the fine, the U.S. District Court for the Northern District of Illinois made clear on August 20, 1993, the Justice Department would have to prove that the Evergreen broadcasts in question indeed were indecent.[78]

On February 23, 1994, this case settled out of court. As part of the settlement, the FCC agreed to drop charges of indecency against Evergreen, along with $39,750 in fines, and to draw up guidelines that will explain the FCC's indecency ban. The report's deadline was November 22, 1994, and at first the FCC was saying the report would be on time.[79] But in early December 1994, an FCC official said that the report would not be ready until January or February 1995.[80] But two years later, in January 1997, the report had still not been released.[81]

Evergreen agreed to drop its counterclaim questioning the constitutionality of the FCC's enforcement of the indecency ban. Evergreen also agreed to pay the FCC $10,000 while not admitting that it engaged in any wrongdoing.[82]

Infinity Broadcasting settled, as well. In June and July of 1995, the U.S. Court of Appeals for the District of Columbia Circuit had upheld the constitutionality of indecency laws and procedures.[83] Infinity was a plaintiff in both of those suits.[84] Less than two months later, on September 1, 1995, the FCC released a report announcing the settlement agreement. The FCC would drop its fines, the report said, and Infinity would make a "voluntary contribution to the U.S. Treasury in the amount of $1,715,000." Infinity also agreed to develop an educational program for all "on-air personnel" and to "issue a policy statement" to them that calls attention to the federal law prohibiting broadcast of indecent speech. But, the report said, "Infinity has not admitted any wrongdoing or liability. Rather, the settlement agreement will end the time consuming litigation that would be required to resolve the outstanding enforcement actions."[85]

FCC Chair Reed Hundt commented in the report that the settlement with Infinity was the largest amount a broadcasting company had ever contributed to the FCC. He said, "The agreement reaffirms the Commission's commitment to enforce the indecency statute and to bring all enforcement proceedings to a just and speedy conclusion."[86] And Commissioner Quello reiterated that he was "encouraged" by Infinity's steps to "train, supervise, and monitor its on-the-air personnel."[87] He emphasized that he was "pleased that the settlement is premised upon the validity of the FCC's rules."

Although the appellate court in *Act V* upheld the FCC's procedures, and although Infinity paid an enormous fine, the FCC's victories were not total. The appellate court in its conclusion to *Act V*, acknowledged that Infinity and the other appellants in the case had raised valid points. The court concluded, "Although the appellants have failed to show that the Commission's administration of the statute is unconstitutional, we cannot fail to acknowledge that the agency's practices could give rise to some of the evils that the appellants claim are already at hand." The court makes this suggestion to any broadcaster who "comes to the grief alleged in this case": "[T]he broadcaster could . . . state that it will not pay the forfeiture unless ordered to do so in district court."[88] In short, the broadcaster could refuse to pay and force the government to go to court to collect.

Why don't more stations protest their fines by refusing to pay, putting the onus on the government to *prove* that Stern's commentary or songs are indecent? One answer is that the FCC not only hands out fines for indecency, but also it hands out licenses to broadcasters.[89] The power to jerk a license is the power to jerk radio stations around. (And, as mentioned before, it can be more expensive to protest than to pay the fine.[90])

On a more positive note for those who dislike FCC's regulation of broadcast indecency, the Supreme Court has ruled that indecency can go out over cable at any hour of the day or night, unfettered by the FCC,[91] and that "dial-a-porn"—indecent, commercial phone messages—cannot be totally banned by Congress.[92]

The bottom line is that indecent music is not totally banned from the airwaves. But at least until more legal battles are won, to safely play, it is "Gonna Wait 'Til the Midnight Hour."

NOTES

1. *In re Enforcement of Prohibitions Against Broadcast Indecency in 18 U.S.C. § 1464*, 7 FCC Rcd 6464 n.4 (1992). The FCC says that this language is "essentially unchanged" from the definition of indecency upheld in *FCC v. Pacifica*, 438 U.S. 726 (1978). *Goodrich Broadcasting, Inc. v. FCC*, 6 FCC Rcd 2178 (1991), 1991 FCC Lexis 2033 at *2.

The definition used to add "at times of the day when there is a reasonable risk that children may be in the audience." Explaining why it dropped that language, the FCC said:

In our recent actions, we treated the nature of the material involved and the time of day that children are in the audience separately because we believe that the question of the time of a "patently offensive" broadcast is more pertinent to channeling and to whether a broadcast is "actionable" . . . than to whether it is indecent. We note, however, that *because the aim of broadcast indecency regulation is to protect children, a violation finding will only be entered if both components of the test are met—i.e. material must be both indecent and broadcast when there is a reasonable risk that children may be in the audience.*

In re Infinity Broadcasting Corp. of Pennsylvania v. FCC, 3 FCC Rcd 930 n.6 (1987), 1987 FCC Lexis 2416, **3 (emphasis added).

2. John Milward says:

The syndication of Stern's morning show is an intriguing counterpoint to the rise of talk radio's other megastar, Rush Limbaugh. Both men are extremely talented broadcasters who define their shows by encouraging a cult of personality. And in these days of temperate discourse, they also share the distinction of being politically incorrect. But where Limbaugh beats a rigorously conservative drum, Stern marches to a decidedly more liberal beat.

John Milward, "Howard Stern Blasts Off: Chicago May Be in for a Rude Awakening from New York Shock Jock," *Chicago Tribune*, North Sports Final Edition, Oct. 2, 1992, Tempo section, p. 1.

3. Richard Zoglin, "Shock Jock; Howard Stern Is Shaking Up Radio—and the FCC—with His Raunchy, Racist, In-Your-Face Talk, But Listeners Seem to Love It," *Time*, Nov. 30, 1992, p. 72.

4. David Savage, "So Far, 'Shock Jock' Stern Has Had Last Word," *Los Angeles Times*, Home Edition, Dec. 15, 1992, p. A5.

5. Arthur Spiegelman, "FCC Fines Howard Stern's Bosses $600,000 for Talking Dirty," *Reuters*, Dec. 18, 1992, AM Cycle. See also "Freedom, Even for Slimeballs," *Star Tribune*, Metro Edition, Dec. 21, 1992, p. 10A.

6. "FCC Considers Fining Infinity," *Daily Variety*, Nov. 30, 1992, p. 16.

7. Jon Pareles, "Radio View: Shock Jocks Shake Up Uncle Sam," *op. cit.*

8. *FCC v. Pacifica*, 438 U.S. 729 (1978).

9. Ibid. at 731–732 (FCC's characterization of language).

10. 18 U.S.C. § 1464 (enacted June 25, 1948) (emphasis added). This statute provides for a fine of up to $10,000 and imprisonment of up to two years.

11. *FCC v. Pacifica*, 438 U.S. 738–741 (1978).

12. *FCC v. Pacifica*, 438 U.S. 748–749 (1978).

13. *Action for Children's Television v. FCC*, 932 F.2d 1504,1506 (D.C. Cir. 1991) This case provides a good history of the FCC and indecency. *Action for Children's Television v. FCC*, 932 F.2d at 1506–1507 (D.C. Cir. 1991).

14. *In re Infinity Broadcasting Corp. of Pennsylvania*, 3 FCC Rcd 930, para. 5, 1987 FCC Lexis 2416 at *6–*7; *Action for Children's Television*, 932 F.2d 1506 (D.C. Cir.

1991). The FCC explained that the narrower standard permitted "anomalous results that could not be justified":

Under that standard, material that portrayed sexual or excretory activities or organs in as patently offensive a manner as the earlier Carlin monologue—and, consequently, of concern with respect to its exposure to children—would have been permissible to broadcast simply because it avoided certain words. That approach, in essence, ignored an entire category of speech by focusing exclusively on specific words rather than the generic definition of indecency. This made neither legal nor policy sense. Accordingly, we concluded that we must take the more difficult approach. . . . [W]e shall use the generic definition of indecency articulated by the Commission in 1975 and approved by the Supreme Court in 1978 as applied to the Carlin monologue.

In re Infinity Broadcasting Corp. of Pennsylvania, 3 FCC Rcd 930, para. 5, 1987 FCC LEXIS 2416 at **6–**7.

15. *In re Infinity Broadcasting Corp. of Pennsylvania*, 3 FCC Rcd 930, para. 4, 1987 FCC Lexis 2416 at **5, (1987); *In re Enforcement of Prohibitions Against Broadcast Indecency in 18 U.S.C. § 1464*, 7 FCC Rcd para. 5 (1992).

16. *In re Infinity Broadcasting Corp. of Pennsylvania*, 3 FCC Rcd 930, para. 5, 1987 FCC Lexis 2416 at **6–**7.

17. April 16, 1987, was also Mark Fowler's last day as FCC chair. Erwin Krasnow, "Government Regulation Persists; Media Audience Is the Victim," *Legal Times*, June 1, 1987, p. 14. See also David Crook and Penny Pagano, "FCC Cracking Down on Radio 'Indecency': KPFK-FM Targeted for Broadcasting an Allegedly Obscene Play About AIDS," *Los Angeles Times*, Home Edition, April 17, 1987, Calendar section, part 6, p. 1.

18. David Crook and Penny Pagano, "FCC Cracking Down"; Caroline E. Mayer, "FCC Curbs Radio, TV Language; Agency Threatens Stations that Are Sexually Explicit," *Washington Post*, Final Edition, April 17, 1987, p. A1. "FCC Tightens Curbs on Language," *Facts on File World News Digest*, April 17, 1987, p. 264 B2; Letta Tayler, "States News Service," April 16, 1987 (available on Lexis/Nexis).

The FCC even referred the matter of the Los Angeles station to the Justice Department for possible prosecution for obscenity. Crook and Pagano, "FCC Cracking Down"; Mayer, "FCC Curbs Radio"; "FCC Tightens Curbs on Language"; Tayler, "States News Service."

The FCC had been receiving roughly 20,000 complaints per year. Mayer, "FCC Curbs Radio"; "FCC Tightens Curbs on Language."

19. *Action for Children's Television v. FCC*, 932 F.2d 1506.

20. "Morality in Media Hails FCC Move," *PR Newswire*, Sept. 26, 1986.

21. *In re Infinity Broadcasting Corp. of Pennsylvania*, 3 FCC Rcd, para. 8 (1987).

Morality in Media is still an active group. Vicki Riley organized a national "Turn Off TV Day" for MIM that was scheduled for November 13, 1992. She explained, "The reason for the Turn Off TV Day is to appeal to the networks [and] prove to them that there are people who are concerned with decency standards." Warren Publishing, Inc., 12 *Communications Daily* 5 (Oct. 26, 1992).

22. "Morality in Media Hails FCC Move." In September 1986, the FCC had sent warning letters to WXRK-FM in New York because of Howard Stern's morning-drive show. It also sent warning letters to KPFK-FM in Los Angeles and to KCSB-FM in Santa Barbara. The FCC had not sent out warning letters since 1978. Alex S. Jones, "FCC Studies 'Indecency' on Radio," *New York Times*, Late City Final Edition, Nov. 22, 1986, p. 9.

23. *Action for Children's Television v. FCC*, 852 F.2d 1332, 1341–1342, 1343 n.18 (D.C. Cir. 1988) (cited in *Action for Children's Television v. FCC*, 932 F.2d 1506–1507).

24. *Action for Children's Television*, 852 F.2d 1344 (cited in *Action for Children's Television*, 932 F.2d 1507).

25. Public Law No. 100–459, § 608, 102 Stat. 2228 (1989) (cited in *Action for Children's Television*, 932 F.2d 1507).

26. Edmund L. Andrews, "The Media Business; Howard Stern Employer Faces $600,000 Fine," *New York Times*, Late City Final Edition, Dec. 18, 1992, p. A1.

27. *Action for Children's Television*, 932 F. 2d 1507.

28. *Action for Children's Television*, 932 F. 2d 508–1509.

29. *Action for Children's Television*, 932 F. 2d 1509–1510. The court relied, in part, on a United States Supreme Court decision that came down in the midst of the proceedings in *Action for Children's Television*. The Supreme Court reiterated the constitutionally protected status of indecent language in striking down a total ban on indecent commercial phone messages—so-called "dial-a-porn." See *Sable Communications v. FCC*, 492 U.S. 115 (1989) (cited in *Action for Children's Television*, 932 F.2d 1507, 1509).

30. Randy Sukow, "House Passes 6 AM-Midnight Indecency Ban; Communications Attorneys Say Provision Will Be Struck Down by Courts," 122 *Broadcasting* 28 (Aug. 10, 1992).

31. Section 16(a) of the Public Telecommunications Act of 1991, Public Law Number 102–356, says:

The Federal Communications Commission shall promulgate regulations to prohibit the broadcasting of indecent programming—
(1) between 6 AM and 10 PM on any day by any public radio station or public television station that goes off the air at or before 12 midnight; and
(2) between 6 AM and 12 midnight on any day for any radio or television broadcast station not described in paragraph (1).

Quoted in *In re Matter of Enforcement of Prohibitions Against Broadcast Indecency in 18 U.S.C. § 1464*, 7 FCC Rcd, para. 1 (1992).

32. *Action for Children's Television v. FCC*, 11 F.3d 170 (D.C. Cir. 1993). For background on the situation leading to the suit, see Bill Holland, "FCC Fines Ill. Stations for Discriminatory Practices," *Billboard*, Oct. 3, 1992, p. 69; Jack Pollack, "Counterpunch: Radio Stations Should Challenge FCC in Court," *Los Angeles Times*, Home Edition, Nov. 9, 1992, Calendar section, p. F3; Dennis Wharton, "'Indecency' Regs Ripped by Groups," *Daily Variety*, Nov. 13, 1992, p. 8; Sukow, "House Passes Indecency Ban."

33. *Action for Children's Television v. FCC*, 11 F.3d 170 (D.C. Cir. 1993).

34. *Action for Children's Television v. FCC*, 58 F.3d 654 (D.C. Cir. 1995).

35. *Action for Children's Television v. FCC*, 59 F.3d 1249, 1252, 1262 (D.C. Cir. 1995).

36. See 47 U.S.C. § 503 (1992) (approved Dec. 5. 1992) and "History; Ancillary Laws and Direction" under said statute.   See also Jube Shiver, Jr., "Federal Fines Rise Sharply; Regulation: Agencies Are Now Collecting about $2 Billion a Year, Thanks Primarily to Expanded Authority," *Los Angeles Times*, Home Edition, Jan. 15, 1993, Business section, p. D1 (saying, not quite accurately, that the FCC can levy penalties of up to $200,000 and that the increase was tenfold).

37. See Letter to Mel Karmazin, 5 FCC Rcd 7291, 7293 (DA 90-1761, Dec. 7, 1990). See also Paul Farhi, "FCC to Levy Stiff Fine Over Stern; Agency Seeks $600,000 from Three Stations," *Washington Post*, Final Edition, Dec. 18, 1992, p. D1. Phyllis Stark, "FCC Ownership Caps, Indecency Fines Made Waves," *Billboard*, Dec. 26, 1992, Radio section, p. 80. See also, Paul Farhi, "FCC's Stern Punishment; Radio Group To Be Fined, Purchases May Be Delayed," *Washington Post*, Final Edition, Nov. 25, 1992, p. E1.

38. "FCC Cleans Out the Pipeline on Indecency," 117 *Broadcasting* 28 (Oct. 30, 1989).

39. Jon Pareles, "Pop View; A Case Against Censoring Rock Lyrics," *New York Times*, Late City Final Edition, May 3, 1987, section 2, p. 22; Letta Tayler, "States News Service."

40. See *In re Liability of Nationwide Communications, Inc.*, 6 FCC Rcd 3695 (DA 90–1510, April 19, 1990). See also Dennis McDougal and Claudia Puig, "Leykis Leads Counterattack Against FCC Fines," *Los Angeles Times*, Home Edition, Oct. 28, 1989, Calendar section, p. F1. See also, Steve Hochman, "Radio 'X'; Popular Rock Groups Often Cross the Line—How Do the Stations Cope?" *Los Angeles Times*, Home Edition, Oct. 17, 1991, Calendar section, p. F1.

41. See *In re Liability of Guy Gannett*, 5 FCC Rcds (DA 90–1846, Dec. 17, 1990). See also, Bill Holland, "Broadcasters Being Showered with Bad News About the Proposed Spectrum," *Billboard*, Jan. 19, 1991, Radio section, p. 22.   See also McDougal and Puig, "Leykis Leads"; Doug Halonen, "FCC Cracks Down on 'Indecent' Radio," *Electronic Media*, Oct. 30, 1989, p. 1.

42. See FCC letter to Legacy Broadcasting, Licensee of WLLZ-FM, 6 FCCR 3698 (DA 90–1643, Sept. 29, 1989).   See also, Doug Halonen, "Detroit FM Fined for 'Indecency,' *Electronic Media*, Oct. 9, 1989, p. 42; Warren Publishing, Inc., *Communications Daily*, FCC Daily Digest section, Oct. 5, 1989.

43. See FCC Letter to Michael J. Faherty, 6 FCCR 3704 (DA 90–1646, Oct. 26, 1989).   *See also* "FCC Cleans Out the Pipeline." See also, "Indecent Broadcasts Lead to FCC Fines on 4 Radio Stations," *New York Times*, Late City Final, Oct. 27, 1989, p. B6.

44. See *In re Evergreen Media Corp.*, 6 FCC Rcd 502 (DA 91–55, Jan. 28, 1991). See also "FCC Fines Chicago Station $6,000 for Indecency," 117 *Broadcasting* 71 (Dec. 11, 1989).

45. See *In re Evergreen Media Corp.*, 6 FCC Rcd, 503.   See also Joe Flint, "WLUP-AM Goes to Court; Station Refused to Pay Indecency Fine in Protest of Decision," 122 *Reed Publishing USA* 10 (Aug. 24, 1992); "FCC Turns Up the Heat."

46. "Littler Deal; Radio Network Regional Advertising Closed Circuit Brief Article," 121 *Broadcasting* 6 (Aug. 5, 1991).

47. See Letter to Carl J. Wagner, 6 FCC Rcd 3692 (DA 90–1502, July 19, 1990).   See also Warren Publishing, Inc., 10 *Communications Daily* 9 (July 25, 1990).

48. See Letter to Carl J. Wagner, 6 FCC Rcd 3692 (DA 90-1502, July 19, 1990).

49. See Letter to KGB Inc., 7 FCC RCD 3207 (FCC 92–223, May 26, 1992).   See also "FCC Hit a New High with Its Indecency Fines; $25,000 Penalty on KGB-FM San Diego," 122 *Broadcasting* 56 (May, 25, 1992); "FCC Keeps New Fines Policy," 32 *Television Digest* 4 (May 25, 1992); Kevin Brass, "2 Lewd Songs Cost KGB-FM a $25,000 Fine," *Los Angeles Times*, San Diego County Edition, May 22, 1992, Calendar section, p. F1.

50. Phyllis Stark with Carrie Borzillo, "CIRK Jock Among Airwaves' Most Wanted? Not!" *Billboard*, Radio section, May 30, 1992, p. 79.

51. See Letter to State University of New York, 8 FCC Rcd 456 (FCC 93-3, Jan. 7, 1993).   See also Warren Publishing, Inc., 33 *Television Digest* 4 (1993); "Short Takes," *Daily Variety*, Jan. 8, 1993, p. 59.

52. See Letter to Evergreen Media, 8 FCC 1266, 1267 (FCC 93–97, Feb. 25, 1993). See also Bill Holland, "WLUP Gets Another Letter from FCC," *Billboard*, March 21, 1992, Radio section, p. 128; "Evergreen to FCC: Let's Talk About Sex," *Billboard*, May 23, 1992, Radio section, p. 69.

53. See Letter to Greater Los Angeles Radio, Inc., 7 FCC Rcs 7321 (FCC 92–481, Oct. 27, 1992). See also Claudia Puig, "KLSX Owner Responds to FCC's Howard Stern Fine," *Los Angeles Times*, Home Edition, Jan. 1, 1992, Calendar section, p. F2.

54. Warren Publishing, Inc., *Communications Daily*, Oct. 26, 1992, p. 5.

55. Kathleen O'Steen, "Stern Speech Must Be Free, ACLU Avows," *Daily Variety*, Dec. 18, 1992, p. 5.

56. "ACLU Protests FCC Fine Against Stern," United Press International, Dec. 17, 1992, BC cycle.

57. Claudia Puig, "Are Kids Listening? Youngsters Speak Out About Radio's King of Raunch: Howard Stern," *Los Angeles Times*, Home Edition, Dec. 21, 1992, Calendar section, p. F1.

58. This author gratefully thanks a graduate student at the University of Missouri School of Journalism, Andrew Flum, for a tape recording of that "Butt Bongo" performance.

59. Christian Wiessner, "Howard Stern Outrages Just About Everyone and He's Proud of It," *Reuters*, Dec. 3, 1992, BC cycle.

60. See Letter to Mel Karmazin, 8 FCC Rcd 2688 (No. FCC 92–554, Dec. 18, 1992). See also, Dennis Wharton, "Infinity Hit with 600G Stern Fine," *Daily Variety*, Dec. 21, 1992, p. 3; Warren Publishing, Inc., "Largest FCC Fine Ever; Infinity Fined Record $600,000 for Stern Broadcasts Ruled Indecent," 12 *Communications Daily* 2 (Dec. 21, 1992); Joe Palka, "Howard Stern's Mouth Puts Bite on Infinity," *The Washington Times*, Final Edition, Dec. 20, 1992, p. D3.

61. See 8 FCC Rcd at 2694. See also King, "Talking Trash," and Edmund L. Andrews, "The Media Business."

62. Joe Palka, *op. cit.* See also, Pat Widder, "'Shock jock' Stern Lands Record Fine for Infinity Broadcasting," *Chicago Tribune*, North Sports Final Edition, Dec. 19, 1992, p. 1.

63. Pat Widder, "'Shock jock' Stern"; Warren Publishing, Inc., "Largest FCC Fine Ever." See also, Susan Bickelhaupt, "FCC Levies Fine Over Stern Antics," *Boston Globe*, City Edition, Dec. 19, 1992, p. 28.

The fine even got the attention of Agence France Presse. "U.S. Broadcasting Board Fines Radio Network for Shock Jock," *Agence France Presse*, Dec. 18, 1992.

64. The Cook Inlet stations are WZLX-FM in Boston, WUSN-FM in Chicago and WZGC-FM in Atlanta. Dennis Wharton, "Shock Jock B'casts May Cost Infinity $750,000," *Daily Variety*, Dec. 10, 1992, p. 1. The Cook Inlet stations are primarily owned by 6,500 native Alaskans. Warren Publishing, Inc., "Largest FCC Fine Ever." See also, "FCC to Fine Radio Stations Record $600,000 over Howard Stern," *Reuters*, Dec. 18, 1992, PM cycle.

65. Warren Publishing, Inc., "Largest FCC Fine Ever," p. 2.

66. Wharton, "Shock jock b'casts."

67. Catherine Applefeld, "FCC Slaps More Fines on Infinity, Approves WIP Sale," *Billboard*, Aug. 28, 1993, p. 83.

68. "Infinity Sees Mixed FCC Success," *Junk Bond Reporter*, Vol. 4, No. 5, Feb. 7, 1994, p. 1.

69. Letter to Agape Broadcasting Foundation, Inc., 9 FCC Rcd 1679 (DA 94–273, April 1, 1994).

70. Letter to Waterman Broadcasting, Corp., 11 FCC Rcd 14547 (DA 96–1858, Nov. 12, 1996).

71. Bill Holland, "Congressional (In)Action Good for Radio; Several Legislative Conflicts Go Broadcasters' Way," *Billboard*, Oct. 15, 1994, p. 96.

72. Bill Holland, "Recession's Effects Resonated in Radio Rule-Making," *Billboard*, Dec. 26, 1992, Radio section, p. 83.

73. See 6 FCC Rcd at 503.   See also Flint, "WLUP-AM Goes to Court," "FCC Turns Up the Heat."

74. Bill Holland, "WLUP Case Seems Court-Bound; Would Be 1st Over Indecency Rules," *Billboard*, Feb. 15, 1992, Radio section, p. 75.

75. Joe Flint, "Evergreen to Fight Indecency Charge: Since It has No Avenue of Appeal for FCC Fine, It Will Refuse to Pay," 122 *Broadcasting* 91 (Jan. 13, 1992).

76. Warren Publishing, Inc., 11 *Communications Daily* 5 (Dec. 9, 1991).

77. Joe Flint, "WLUP-AM Goes to Court." In the meantime, the FCC sent Evergreen a letter of inquiry about broadcasts made in January 1991 over WLUP. The FCC again, in part, didn't like some music—new lyrics to the song "Venus." In its response to the FCC inquiry, Evergreen even included a videotape of segments of news events such as the Clarence Thomas confirmation hearings and of the Donahue show. Evergreen's attorney thereby hoped to demonstrate that "contemporary community standards include sexual themes."   Bill Holland, "Bush Ban on Indecent Radio Being Challenged," *Billboard*, Sept. 12, 1992, p. 82.

78. *United States v. Evergreen Media Corp.*, 832 F. Supp. 1183, 1187 (N.D. Ill. 1993). *See also* Bill Holland, "NAB Gears Up to Fight Performance Right; Recording Industry Wants Copyright Law Changed," *Billboard*, March 13, 1993, p. 111; Bill Holland, "Bush Ban."

79. "Expect the FCC's indecency rules guideline report to make it to the commissioners' offices by the deadline date of Nov. 22, a commission spokesman says."   Bill Holland, "FCC Indecency Guideline Report on Schedule," *Billboard*, Nov. 12, 1994, p. 101.

80. Bill Holland, "FCC Delays Indecency Paper Again, Plans Winter Release," *Billboard*, Dec. 3, 1994, p. 100.

81. In a January 23, 1997 telephone interview, a spokesperson from the FCC Mass Media Bureau confirmed that the report had never been issued. He cited the problem of "limited resources" at the FCC. The report, according to the spokesperson, "would cite cases and sanctions that have been imposed" by the FCC in order to "provide guidance."

82. "Recent Cases," *Entertainment Law Reporter*, Vol. 16, No. 4, Sep. 1994; See also James Warren, "FCC to Void Fines for WLUP's Owner," *Chicago Tribune*, North Sports Final Edition, Feb. 23, 1994, p. 3, Zone N.

83. See *Action for Children's Television v. FCC* cases at 58 F.3d 654 (D.C. Cir. 1995) and 59 F.3d 1249 (D.C. Cir. 1995).

84. Ibid.

85. "Mass Media Action Commission Settles Indecency Proceedings Involving Infinity Broadcasting Corporation," Report No. MM 95–89, Sep. 1, 1995. See also Anthony Ramirez, "$1.7 Million to End Howard Stern Indecency Case," *New York Times*, Late City Final Edition, Sept. 2, 1995, p. 33.

86. Ibid.

87. Ibid.

88. 59 F.3d at 1261.

89. See, *e.g.,* Pollack, "Counterpunch."

90. Ibid.

91. *Jones v. Wilkinson*, 800 F.2d 989 (10th Cir. 1986), *aff'd*, 480 U.S. 926 (1987). For an editorial on the difference in the legal standards applied to cable stations and broadcast stations, see Edmund L. Andrews, "2 Views of Decency," *New York Times*, Late Edition, Dec. 28, 1992, p. A12.

92. See *Sable Communications v. FCC*, 492 U.S. 115 (1989) (cited in *Action for Children's Television v. FCC*, 932 F.2d at 1507, 1509).

APPENDIX: FCC PROCEDURE IN HANDING OUT FINES

If a group wants to "clean the air," here is the typical process it follows, along with the FCC's procedure and the radio stations' recourse:

1. The FCC's "Mass Media Bureau" handles complaints and ultimately issues fines.[1] A complaint filed by a listener with the FCC is directed to the enforcement division's investigations branch. The complaint lands on the desk of an investigator at the FCC annex at 2025 M Street in Washington, D.C.[2]
2. The investigator makes the first cut, deciding which complaints are meritless and which deserve further attention. Substantiating material (tapes, transcripts) are imperative.[3] Because the FCC receives so many thousands of complaints, it can only process the relatively few accompanied by substantiating tapes or transcripts.[4] For instance, in the six-month period prior to March 1992, the FCC received 53 substantiated complaints.[5]
3. An attorney for the investigations branch reviews the investigator's determination on the complaint.
4. The determination on the complaint is forwarded to an assistant chief of the Mass Media Bureau for review by that assistant chief and one of the General Counsel's deputies.[6]
5. The determination on the complaint is presented at a regular monthly meeting of aides of the commissioners.
6. The final determination is made by the commissioners, who are counseled by their aides. The process to this point takes almost one year.
7. A letter or notice is issued with signatures by the Mass Media Bureau.[7] Usually, a "letter of inquiry" is the first step.[8] The Mass Media Bureau usually waits for a response by the station before proceeding to the forfeiture (fine) stage, thus avoiding a "verdict first, trial later" procedure.[9]
8. The next step is a "notice of apparent liability for forfeitures" (NAL) issued by the Mass Media Bureau.
9. The final step by the Mass Media Bureau is a "notice of forfeiture," or fine.[10]
10. After receiving a notice of forfeiture, a station has 30 days to respond.[11]
11. A station may not appeal the fine to the U.S. Court of Appeals because the Communications Act does not provide for appeal of the fine.[12] A station may ask for reconsideration of the fine, but the Mass Media Bureau does not have to reconsider the fine. (For instance, Evergreen's request for reconsideration was denied).[13] The station's only recourse is to pay the fine—or refuse to pay the fine.[14] (NOTE: Broadcast stations can appeal actions other than fines to the U.S. Court of Appeals for the District of Columbia Circuit.[15])
12. If a station refuses to pay a fine, then the FCC can refer the matter to the Justice Department, which has to take the station to court.[16] The Justice Department sues in the district court where the station legally resides.

APPENDIX: STATUTES ON INDECENCY

[The following statutory provision authorizes criminal penalties for broadcasting indecency. Note that persons convicted under the statute can spend two years in jail, but can only be fined $10,000.]

Title 18 United States Code

§ 1464. Broadcasting obscene language

Whoever utters any obscene, indecent, or profane language by means of radio communication shall be fined not more than $10,000 or imprisoned not more than two years, or both.

[The following statutory provisions control the FCC and broadcasters in relation to indecency. Although these statutes do not authorize jail time, they do authorize $250,000 fines.]

Title 47 United States Code

§ 312. Administrative sanctions

(a) **Revocation of station license or construction permit.** The Commission may revoke any station license or construction permit—

. . .

(3) for willful or repeated failure to operate substantially as set forth in the license;

(4) for willful or repeated violation of, or willful or repeated failure to observe any provision of this Act or any rule or regulation of the Commission authorized by this Act or by a treaty ratified by the United States;

(5) for violation of or failure to observe any final cease and desist order issued by the Commission under this section;

(6) for violation of section . . . 1464 of title 18 of the United States Code;

. . .

(b) **Cease and desist orders.** Where any person (1) has failed to operate substantially as set forth in a license, (2) has violated or failed to observe any of the provisions of this Act, or section . . . 1464 of title 18 of the United States Code . . . , or (3) has violated or failed to observe any rule or regulation of the Commission authorized by this Act or by a treaty ratified by the United States, the Commission may order such person to cease and desist from such action.

(c) **Order to show cause.** Before revoking a license or permit pursuant to subsection (a), or issuing a cease and desist order pursuant to subsection (b), the Commission shall serve upon the licensee, permittee, or person involved an order to show cause why an order of revocation or a cease and desist order should not be issued. Any such order to show cause shall contain a statement of the matters with respect to which the Commission is inquiring and shall call upon said licensee, permittee, or person to appear here before the Commission at a time and place stated in the order, but in no event less than thirty days after the receipt of such order, and give evidence upon the matter specified therein; except that where safety of life or property is involved, the Commission may provide in the order for a shorter period. If after hearing, or a waiver thereof, the Commission determines that an order of revocation or a cease and desist order should issue, it shall issue such order, which shall include a statement of the findings of the Commission and the grounds and reasons therefor and specify the effective date of the order, and shall cause the same to be served on said licensee, permittee, or person.

(d) Burden of proof. In any case where a hearing is conducted pursuant to the provisions of this section, both the burden of proceeding with the introduction of evidence and the burden of proof shall be upon the Commission.

. . .

[The following statutes say that decisions by the FCC can be appealed to the federal court of appeals in Washington, D.C. From there, appeals can go to the Supreme Court. But these statutes do not allow for the appeal of fines. Because a broadcasting company cannot appeal a fine, it can only refuse to pay the fine, thus forcing the Justice Department to sue for collection. But if the Justice Department sues, it must sue the broadcaster in a federal trial court in the broadcaster's geographical area. And the Justice Department must prove that the broadcaster aired material that is indecent. That gives the broadcaster the opportunity to argue that the material is not indecent.

The statute of indecency is one year. This means that any broadcaster who has not been notified within a year that a broadcast was indecent is off the hook.]

Title 47 United States Code

§ 402. Judicial review of Commission's orders and decisions

(a) Procedure. Any proceeding to enjoin, set aside, annul or suspend any order of the Commission under this Act (except those appealable under subsection (b) of this section) shall be brought as provided by and in the manner prescribed in . . . [28 USC §§ 2341 et seq.].[17]

(b) Right to appeal. Appeals may be taken from decisions and orders of the Commission to the United States Court of Appeals for the District of Columbia in any of the following cases:

(1) By any applicant for a construction permit or station license, whose application is denied by the Commission.

(2) By any applicant for the renewal or modification of any such instrument of authorization whose application is denied by the Commission.

. . .

(5) By the holder of any construction permit or station license which has been modified or revoked by the Commission.

(6) By any other person who is aggrieved or whose interests are adversely affected by any order of the Commission granting or denying any application described in paragraphs (1) [and] (2). . . .

(7) By any person upon whom an order to cease and desist has been served under section 312 of this Act.[18]

(8) By any radio operator whose license has been suspended by the Commission.

. . .

(h) Remand. In the event that the court shall render a decision and enter an order reversing the order of the Commission, it shall remand the case to the Commission to carry out the judgment of the court and it shall be the duty of the Commission, in the absence of the proceedings to review such judgment, to forthwith give effect thereto, and unless otherwise ordered by the court, to do so upon the basis of the proceedings already had and the record upon which said appeal was heard and determined.

. . .

(j) Finality of decision; review by Supreme Court. The court's judgment shall be final, subject, however, to review by the Supreme Court of the United States. . . .

§ 503. Forfeitures *[Fines]*

. . .

(b) Activities constituting violations authorizing imposition of forfeiture penalty; amount of penalty; procedures applicable; persons subject to penalty; liability exemption period.

(1) Any person who is determined by the Commission, in accordance with paragraph (3) or (4) of this subsection, to have—

(A) willfully or repeatedly failed to comply substantially with the terms and conditions of any license, permit, certificate, or other instrument or authorization issued by the Commission;

(B) willfully or repeatedly failed to comply with any of the provisions of this Act or of any rule, regulation, or order issued by the Commission under this Act or under any treaty, convention, or other agreement to which the United States is a party and which is binding upon the United States;

. . .

(D) violated any provision of section . . . 1464 of title 18, United States Code;[19] shall be liable to the United States for a forfeiture penalty. . . .

(2) (A) If the violator is (i) a broadcast station licensee or permittee, (ii) a cable television operator, or (iii) an applicant for any broadcast or cable television operator license, permit, certificate, or other instrument or authorization issued by the Commission, the amount of any forfeiture penalty determined under this section shall not exceed $25,000 for each violation or each day of a continuing violation, except that the amount assessed for any continuing violation shall not exceed a total of $250,000 for any single act or failure to act described in paragraph (1) of this subsection.

. . .

(D) The amount of such forfeiture penalty shall be assessed by the Commission, or its designee, by written notice. In determining the amount of such a forfeiture penalty, the Commission or its designee shall take into account the nature, circumstances, extent, and gravity of the violation and, with respect to the violator, the degree of culpability, any history of prior offenses, ability to pay, and such other matters as justice may require.

(3) (A) At the discretion of the Commission, a forfeiture penalty may be determined against a person under this subsection after notice and an opportunity for a hearing

before the Commission or an administrative law judge thereof. . . . Any person against whom a forfeiture penalty is determined under this paragraph may obtain review thereof pursuant to section 402(a).[20]

(B) If any person fails to pay an assessment of a forfeiture penalty determined under subparagraph (A) of this paragraph, after it has become a final and unappealable order or after the appropriate court has entered final judgment in favor of the Commission, the Commission shall refer the matter to the Attorney General of the United States, who shall recover the amount assessed in any appropriate district court of the United States. In such action, the validity and appropriateness of the final order imposing the forfeiture penalty shall not be subject to review.

(4) Except as provided in paragraph (3) of this subsection, no forfeiture penalty shall be imposed under this subsection against any person unless and until—

(A) the Commission issues a notice of apparent liability, in writing, with respect to such person;

(B) such notice has been received by such person, or until the Commission has sent such notice to the last known address of such person, by registered or certified mail; and

(C) such person is granted an opportunity to show, in writing, within such reasonable period of time as the Commission prescribes by rule or regulation, why no such forfeiture penalty should be imposed.

Such a notice shall (i) identify each specific provision, term, and condition of any Act, rule, regulation, order, treaty, convention, or other agreement, license, permit, certificate, instrument, or authorization which such person apparently violated or with which such person apparently failed to comply; (ii) set forth the nature of the act or omission charged against such person and the facts upon which such charge is based; and (iii) state the date on which such conduct occurred. Any forfeiture penalty determined under this paragraph shall be recoverable pursuant to section 504(a) of this Act.

. . .

(6) No forfeiture penalty shall be determined or imposed against any person under this subsection if—

(A) such person holds a broadcast station license . . . and if the violation charged occurred—

(I) more than 1 year prior to the date of issuance of the required notice or notice of apparent liability;[21] . . .

. . .

§ 504. Forfeitures

(a) Recovery. The forfeitures provided for in this Act shall be payable into the Treasury of the United States, and shall be recoverable, except as otherwise provided with respect to a forfeiture penalty determined under section 503(b)(3) of this Act,[22] in a civil suit in the name of the United States brought in the district where the person or carrier has its principal operating office or in any district through which the line or system of the carrier runs: Provided, That any suit for the recovery of a forfeiture imposed pursuant to the provisions of this Act shall be a trial de novo. . . . Such forfeitures shall be in addition to any other general or specific, penalties herein provided. It shall be the duty of the various district attorneys [U.S. attorneys], under the direction of the Attorney General of the United States, to prosecute for the recovery of forfeitures under this Act. The costs and expenses of such prosecutions shall be paid from the appropriation for the expenses of the courts of the United States.

. . .

NOTES

1. Bill Holland and Phyllis Stark, "FCC Slaps Indecency Fines on Three Stern Outlets," *Billboard*, Oct. 31, 1992, p. 4.

2. Joe Flint, "The Case for Raising Caps; Ownership of Radio and Television Stations," 122 *Broadcasting* 23 (Aug. 31, 1992)

3. Flint, "Raising Caps."

4. Harry A. Jessell, "FCC Puts Broadcasters on Notice for Indecency," 122 *Broadcasting* 29 (1992).

5. Jessell, "Broadcasters on Notice."

6. Flint, "Raising Caps."

7. Ibid.

8. Jessell, "Broadcasters on Notice."

9. "97.1 KLSX Responds to FCC Threat of Fine," *Business Wire*, Jan. 4, 1993 (quoting KLSX general manager Jim Freeman).

10. Jessell, "Broadcasters on Notice."

11. Joe Palka, "Howard Stern's Mouth Puts Bite on Infinity," *Washington Times*, Final Edition, Dec. 20, 1992, p. D3; Warren Publishing, Inc., "Largest FCC Fine Ever; Infinity Fined Record $600,000 for Stern Broadcasts Ruled Indecent," 12 *Communications Daily* 2 (Dec. 21, 1992).

12. See 47 U.S.C. § 402 (1992); Joe Flint, "WLUP; AM Goes to Court; Station Refused to Pay Indecency Fine in Protest of Decision," 122 *Reed Publishing USA* 10 (Aug. 24, 1992); "FCC May Go to Court Against Chicago Station," *United Press International*, Feb. 6, 1992, BC cycle.

13. Flint, "WLUP."

14. Bill Holland, "WLUP Case Seems Court-Bound; Would Be 1st Over Indecency Rules," *Billboard*, Feb. 15, 1992, Radio section, p. 75; Joe Flint, "Evergreen to Fight Indecency Charge; Since It has No Avenue of Appeal for FCC Fine, It Will Refuse to Pay; Matter then Gets Handed Over to Justice Department," 122 *Broadcasting* 91 (Jan. 13, 1992).

15. See 47 U.S.C. § 402(b) (1992) for a list of FCC actions that are so appealable. See also, *e.g.*, *Action for Children's Television v. FCC*, 932 F.2d 1504 (1991); *Action for Children's Television v. FCC*, 821 F.2d 741 (1987).

16. Flint, "Evergreen"; "FCC May Go to Court." See also, Warren Publishing, Inc., 11 *Communications Daily*, Dec. 9, 1991.

17. Title 28 United States Code § 2341. Definitions

. . .

(3) "agency" means—

(A) The Commission, when the order sought to be reviewed was entered by the Federal Communications Commission. . . .

§ 2342. Jurisdiction of court of appeals

The court of appeals (other than the United States Court of Appeals for the Federal Circuit) has exclusive jurisdiction to enjoin, set aside, suspend (in whole or in part), or to determine the validity of—
(1) all final orders of the Federal Communications Commission made reviewable by section 402(a) of title 47. . . .

18. See Title 47 United States Code § 312 reprinted on pp. 67–68.
19. See Title 18 United States Code § 1464, reprinted on p. 67.
20. See Title 47 United States Code § 402(a), reprinted on p. 68.
21. This provision establishes a statute of limitations upon the FCC. If it does not act within this time period, then it is barred from taking action against the license holder.
22. See Title 47 United States Code § 503(b)(3), reprinted on pp. 69–70.

6

Music Lyrics: As Censored as They Wanna Be

Jeffrey L. L. Stein

> *People* magazine said that 2-Live Crew's album *As Nasty as They Wanna Be*, which lasts 80 minutes, uses the word "fuck" 226 times, has 87 descriptions of oral sex, and at least one mention of incest. The album refers to women as "bitches" and "whores" 163 times.
>
> —*People* magazine, July 2, 1990, p. 84.

The effects of rock 'n' roll music, the upstart musical genre that many said would never last, have been present for more than 40 years. Throughout that time, American "society" has criticized the forms that popular music has taken as the nation itself changed with the music.

In the 1950s, the pelvic gyrations of Elvis Presley were censored from network television. In the 1960s, as the British invasion hit America's shores a generation of youth changed its hairstyle and listening habits. Low-cut shirts, white suits, and gold chains were the rage as the pounding disco beat dominated the 1970s. Then came the country music boom of the early 1980s and the early 1990s. For more than a decade, MTV has brought the dimension of sight to the sound the public had become used to, and younger and younger consumers have been exposed to more varieties of rock 'n' roll than ever before.

Now more than ever, concern surrounds the lyrics of certain popular songs. The music industry bowed to public pressure in the late 1980s and agreed to voluntarily place warning labels on products containing lyrics that might offend some listeners. But those labels are not enough for some. The popularity of rap music has led many to call for a complete ban of certain songs or records. The graphic and explicit lyrics of many of these songs, including 2-Live Crew's "As Nasty as They Wanna Be," have led to intervention by law-enforcement authorities trying to ban distribution of this music.

To date, these efforts have resulted in little more than some legal battles that have only briefly interfered with the artists' efforts. Ironically, they also have directly led to a greater interest in the music itself, music that might have gone largely unnoticed. Most Americans had never heard of 2-Live Crew until Broward County, Florida, tried to ban distribution of the group's music, creating the most public attempt at censorship in recent memory.

Music is considered speech[1] and as such is protected by the First Amendment, which states that "Congress shall make no law abridging freedom of speech." The ban on limiting freedom of speech also extends to the individual states through the Fourteenth Amendment.

Therefore, the presumption is that speech, including music, is protected and cannot be limited by government. The ability to express one's self, free from government retribution, is fundamental to our democratic system. However, the First Amendment does have some limitations. One limitation is obscenity. There is no constitutional protection for speech that is termed obscene.

Material determined to be obscene can be banned in accordance with standards developed by the U.S. Supreme Court in the 1973 case of *Miller v. California.*[2] (See Appendix following this chapter on the Brief History of Legal Tests for Obscenity and Appendix on the Federal Statutes Relating to Obscenity.) The high Court's *Miller* test provides for flexibility as times change, allows "artistic" material to be excluded from censorship, and permits individual communities and states to have some say over material that may be banned locally.

Under a Florida obscenity statute, officials tried to ban the selling of "As Nasty as They Wanna Be." Before this case, there apparently had never been an obscenity challenge to a musical composition containing both words and lyrics.[3]

While one may be seemingly hard-pressed to demonstrate that mere music without lyrics would be obscene, in a pre-*Miller* case, the U.S. Supreme Court refused to hear the appeal of an individual convicted of obscenity for sending music-only phonograph records and labels through the mail.[4]

Luke Records, Inc. v. Navarro is the case involving 2-Live Crew. Nick Navarro is the Sheriff in Broward County, Florida, who sought 2-Live Crew's conviction. In this case, the district court failed to follow the *Miller* standards properly. As a result, the U.S. Court of Appeals for the Eleventh Circuit threw out the Florida district court's original judgment that "As Nasty as They Wanna Be" was obscene.[5]

For a court to find the material to be obscene, all three prongs of the *Miller* test have to be shown independently. A work is obscene if:

1. the average person, applying contemporary community standards, would find that the work, taken as a whole, appeals to the prurient interest;
2. the work depicts or describes, in a patently offensive way, sexual conduct specifically defined by the applicable state law; and
3. the work as a whole lacks serious literary, artistic, political or scientific value.[6]

At the district court level in 2-Live Crew's case, the state introduced only one piece of evidence: a cassette tape of the group's album. No additional evidence, such as expert witness testimony, was included to support the state's claim that the tape was obscene. The appellate court ruled that the state failed to carry its burden of proving all three elements of the *Miller* obscenity test. The appellate court said the state failed to submit specific evidence defining the "contemporary community standards" in Broward County, Florida. The state also failed to introduce evidence of how the 2-Live Crew recording appealed to the "prurient interest" and how the recording lacked the requisite "serious artistic value." By contrast, 2-Live Crew's counsel introduced various expert-witness testimony showing that the tape did not appeal to the average person's prurient interest and that rap music did have the necessary "serious artistic value," including the fact that, as a recent development, there is a Grammy award presented for rap music.[7]

The trier of fact was a federal district court judge rather than a jury. The judge relied on his own knowledge to define both what the "community standards" at issue would be and to determine if the recording lacked "serious artistic value." The judge had declared that the "community" was three counties for purposes of determining whether 2-Live Crew's album appealed to prurient interests and was patently offensive according to community standards.

Evidence such as expert testimony is not required in obscenity cases. In fact, sometimes "the best evidence is the material, which 'can and does speak for itself,'"[8] especially when the material in question is not within the experience of the average person, such as a juror. It was this "best evidence" authority that the district court judge relied on in determining that he could judge whether the material offended community standards or lacked "value."

The appellate court ruled that it was not necessary to determine whether the judge accurately knew what the "community standards" were. Instead, the appellate court focused on the final *Miller* prong—the "SLAPS" test of whether the work lacks "serious literary, artistic, political or scientific" value. As the appellate court discussed, the Supreme Court has declared that the question of serious value should be decided by a "reasonable person" standard and not by "contemporary community standards."[9] To use community standards would be to subject the work to being judged "solely by the amount of acceptance it has won within a given community;"[10] unpopular material would run the risk of being found to be without value. Thus, as long as the material has some value to some element of the population, the public cannot be denied access to it through obscenity law.

In the 2-Live Crew case, the state failed to introduce any evidence proving that the group's music contained no serious artistic value. Further, the state failed to contradict the evidence presented by 2-Live Crew's counsel, who argued that the music did have the necessary "value." But the trial judge, relying solely on his own knowledge of the community, determined that there was no value to the music and that it was therefore obscene. This decision, the appellate court said, was impermissible: "We reject the argument that simply by listening to this musical work, the judge could determine that it had no serious artistic value."[11] The appellate court reversed the lower court ruling.

One should not be fooled, however, into assuming that because the appeals court ruled the material was not obscene in this case, artists have a free ride to produce whatever they choose. So long as evidence demonstrates that the work has artistic value, the state cannot prove all three of the *Miller* standards and the courts cannot label the material obscene. But if the state can show that material fails the three *Miller* standards, the courts can find the material to be obscene and can therefore ban it.

In the case of 2-Live Crew, one of the concerns expressed by Florida authorities was the effect the music would have on juveniles. It has been long-settled in American law that different standards apply regarding the accessibility of material to juveniles or to adults. What is proper for adults may not be proper for children. This difference in standards results in part from the belief that the government has an interest in protecting its youth from being subjected to some material that willing adults should have the right to hear or see. In other words, a "variable" standard of obscenity prevails in American law: Material that might be obscene for minors might be acceptable for adults.[12]

Note that adults can only be barred from material judged to be legally obscene in accordance with the *Miller* standards. So while authorities may properly prohibit juveniles from accessing certain material that would be merely indecent for adults, authorities must be careful not to encroach on the rights of adults in the process. For example, banning indecent material totally from a bookstore or record store because juveniles happen to be there has been found to be too broad an action. But regulating where the material is kept—requiring it, for instance, to be stored out of the reach of children—is permissible.[13]

Besides flexibility in determining what may be obscene for children as opposed to adults, the law also gives flexibility to different states in determining what is obscene for adults.

According to *Miller*, to be obscene the material must relate to "sexual conduct specifically defined by the *applicable state law*."[14] This wording allows each state to define specifically the conduct that it terms to be "obscene." Also, the Court allows "contemporary *community* standards" to prevail in determining both what material "appeals to the prurient interest" and is "patently offensive."[15] This lack of a uniform, national standard allows different areas of the country to have different definitions of obscenity based on their own tastes and needs.

But it is this very flexibility that can create problems in this age of "mass" mass communication. For example, many radio stations are airing programming from a single satellite source, meaning that the same programming is heard all across the country. Cable-television music channels, including MTV, also program nationally. What problems could result from different states having different standards as to what is proper and what is illegal? Does it matter that one must specifically order cable television but that the radio station signals traveling through the "public" airwaves are more invasive? The very regulatory authority of the Federal Communication Commission (FCC) depends on this "invasive" argument as well as the "scarcity of the frequency spectrum" available for programming.

The Internet has created an interesting issue regarding obscenity law. A man in Memphis downloaded obscenity from a bulletin board in California advertised as "The Nastiest Place on Earth."[16] The operators of the bulletin board system, Robert and Carleen Thomas, were convicted in Memphis, using Memphis "community standards," of violating federal obscenity laws. Both the trial court and the appellate court rejected the argument that the Internet comprised a separate community.[17] Of course, music as well as words and pictures can be transmitted over the Internet.

It seems unlikely that the battle over music and its effects on society will ever be resolved. Some element of music will always grate on the interests or tastes of the majority.

But the rights of the "best" of us are only assured by the rights afforded to the "worst" of us. Our ability to produce anything is only as good as the freedom granted to those who produce unpopular material, which pushes society's tolerance to the limit. As stated, the *Miller* rules are relatively clear and easy to follow; they actually ban from public consumption very little material. We have yet to fully deal with the problems that can arise from "global" and "mass" communication, but it appears that American courts have consistently allowed rock 'n' roll artists the freedom to express themselves as they choose—with the shield of the First Amendment to protect them.

NOTES

1. *Ward v. Rock Against Racism*, 491 U.S. 781 (1989).
2. 413 U.S. 15 (1973).
3. *Luke Records, Inc. v. Navarro*, 960 F.2d 134, 135 (11th Cir. 1992).
4. Ibid. at 135 (citing *United States v. Davis*, 384 U.S. 953 (1966)).
5. See generally *Luke Records, Inc., v. Navarro*, 960 F.2d 134.
6. *Miller v. California*, 413 U.S. 15, 25 (1973).
7. *Luke Records*, 960 F.2d 134, 136.
8. Ibid. at 137.
9. Ibid. at 138, citing with authority *Pope v. Illinois*, 481 U.S. 497 (1987).
10. Ibid.
11. Ibid. at 139.
12. See *New York v. Ferber*, 458 U.S. 747, 756 (1982). See generally *Sable Communications of California v. FCC*, 492 U.S. 115 (1989); *Ginsberg v. New York*, 390 U.S. 629 (1968); *Action for Children's Television v. FCC*, 932 F.2d 1504 (D.C. Cir. 1991).
13. *American Booksellers v. Webb*, 919 F.2d 1493 (11th Cir. 1990).
14. *Miller*, 413 U.S. 15, 25 (emphasis added).
15. Ibid.
16. *United States v. Thomas*, 74 F.3d 701, 705 (6th Cir. 1996).
17. *United States v. Thomas*, 74 F.3d 701, 710–711.

APPENDIX: OBSCENITY

THE LEGAL FRAMEWORK

What is obscenity? The Supreme Court has had difficulty trying to define it. In 1964, Justice Potter Stewart confessed that he did not know how to define *obscenity*, but he added, "I know it when I see it."[1] In 1968, Justice Harlan commented, "The subject of obscenity has produced a variety of views among the members of the Court unmatched in any other course of constitutional adjudication."[2] Indeed, when the Supreme Court devised the current test for obscenity in 1973, Justice Burger admitted that a majority of the Court had not been able to agree on a definition of *obscenity* since 1957.[3]

A BRIEF HISTORICAL PERSPECTIVE

The United States has been grappling with obscenity laws since 1842, when a tariff act banned "importation of all indecent and obscene" paintings and photographs. During the Civil War, in 1865, Congress passed the first law outlawing the mailing of obscene matter in the North because Union soldiers were reading such scandalous books as *Fanny Hill*, also known as *Memoirs of a Woman of Pleasure*, by John Cleland. In 1873, Anthony Comstock, a moral crusader from New York, helped push the first national obscenity bill through Congress by using the slogan of "Morals, not Art or Literature."

Mailing obscene matter remains illegal today. The current statute says, in part, "Every obscene, lewd, lascivious, indecent, filthy or vile article, matter, thing, device or substance . . . [is] declared to be nonmailable matter." A person convicted of mailing anything obscene can be fined $5,000 and imprisoned for up to five years for a first offense; maximum penalties for a second offense are doubled.[4] The problem, of course, is that the statute simply strings together a group of unclear adjectives—"obscene, lewd, lascivious, indecent, or vile." Courts have had the task of trying to interpret such unclear language.

A brief history of the evolving interpretation by U.S. courts of what qualifies as obscene must start with an English rule or test for obscenity devised by Lord Chief Justice Cockburn. The *Hicklin* test, from the 1868 English case of *Regina v. Hicklin*,[5] was whether the tendency of the material is to corrupt minds that are "open to such immoral influences." But a problem with the test was that banning material with a tendency to corrupt minds that are open to immoral influences could mean banning everyone from seeing or reading what might have an affect only on abnormal adults or on children. The U.S. courts added a twist to this rule, making a bad rule worse. The American addition was the "partly obscene" test: If any part of a work was obscene—if any part had a tendency to corrupt minds that are open to immoral influences—then the whole work could be considered obscene.

In 1933, a judge in a New York federal district court, Judge Woolsey, departed from the *Hicklin* test. Customs officials did not want the novel *Ulysses* by James

Joyce coming into the United States. Judge Woolsey read the stream-of-conscious-ness book as a whole and ruled that it was not obscene. Instead, he called the work "a serious experiment in a new . . . literary genre."[6] He judged the book's effect on reasonable adults, not children or abnormal adults, and thus his approach marked an alternative to the *Hicklin* approach.

The Supreme Court overruled the *Hicklin* test in 1957 in the first landmark U.S. Supreme Court decision on obscenity, *Roth v. United States*.[7] Justice Brennan, author of the Court's opinion, wrote that "sex and obscenity are not synonymous." In fact, according to the Court, "Sex, a great and mysterious motive force in human life, has indisputably been a subject of absorbing interest to mankind through the ages; it is one of the vital problems of human interest and public concern." Then the Court turned to the *Hicklin* test and expressly overruled it. "The *Hicklin* test," the Court said, "might well encompass material legitimately treating with sex, and so it must be rejected as unconstitutionally restrictive of the freedoms of speech and press." The Court formulated a new test for obscenity: "Whether to the average person, applying contemporary community standards, the dominant theme of the material taken as a whole appeals to prurient interest."[8]

In *Roth*, the Court formally addressed an important question: "Whether obscenity is utterance within the area of protected speech and press." The Court made explicit what it said it had always assumed, that obscenity is not protected by the First Amendment. Obscenity lacks protection because it is "utterly without redeeming social importance."[9] But on the other hand, "All ideas having even the slightest redeeming social importance . . . have the full protection of the [First Amendment] guaranties, unless . . . they encroach upon the limited area of more important interests."

The *Roth* decision also declared that both federal and California state anti-obscenity laws were valid exercises of governmental police power and that their obscenity laws were not unconstitutionally vague. Although the Court recognized that terms such as "obscene, lewd, lascivious, or filthy" were not "precise," the Court ruled that the laws did not fail to give "adequate notice of what is prohibited."[10]

Almost a decade later, the Court emphasized the "without redeeming social importance" language of *Roth* in a case involving *Fanny Hill*.[11] This book had been involved in one of the first obscenity cases in this country in Massachusetts in 1821, and it was back in court in 1966, attacked by Massachusetts, as well as New York, New Jersey, and Illinois. A plurality[12] of the Court ruled that a book "cannot be proscribed unless it is found to be utterly without redeeming social value."

Peddlers of pornography latched onto the "without redeeming social value" language. For instance, some XXX-rated movies concluded with a discussion of the social significance of the movie. Obscenity law had a large loop-hole.

The Supreme Court seemed preoccupied with the question the English court had wrestled with nearly a century earlier in *Regina v. Hicklin*. What is obscenity? It was not until 1973 that the Supreme Court squarely faced the question that is at the heart of other areas of First Amendment decisions: What state interests justify restraint?

Even Justice Brennan, who had written the opinion in *Roth*, was ready for a change. Brennan wrote, "I am convinced that [the *Roth* approach] cannot bring stability to this area of the law without jeopardizing fundamental First Amendment values, and I have concluded that the time has come to make a significant departure."[13] In part, changing times and attitudes toward sex dictated that the Court back off from trying to define obscenity and get on with the business of answering the more important question of delineating state interests that justify restraint. The Court decided *Roth* in the 1950s, when television portrayed married couples sleeping in twin beds, lyrics to popular songs were tame, and nude love scenes did not appear in critically acclaimed movies. But by 1973, the United States had gone through the Vietnam War, with protests, "free love," and even a nude musical, *Hair*, playing on Broadway. In short, attitudes toward portrayals of sexual matters had changed. In the face of these changes, the Court was becoming more and more divided on obscenity matters.

The 1966 *Fanny Hill* plurality decision was the last time the Court came close to being able to agree on a definition of obscenity.[14] In 1967, the Supreme Court openly admitted in a short opinion that it could not come to agreement on what standard to apply in trying to decide if magazines featuring pictures of nude women were obscene.[15] Because it could not agree on what constituted obscenity, the court reversed a dozen obscenity convictions that year. In 1968, it reversed another dozen.[16] In 1971, the Supreme Court reversed an offensive conduct conviction of a man arrested outside the Los Angeles County Courthouse for wearing a jacket displaying the words "Fuck the Draft."   Writing for the Court, Justice Harlan said, "While the particular four-letter word being litigated here is perhaps more distasteful than most others of its genre, it is nevertheless often true that one man's vulgarity is another's lyric."[17] In short, the Court was recognizing the highly subjective nature of obscenity.

There was another very practical matter that the Court was considering: Roughly 5 percent of its time was being spent on obscenity cases. The Court had become weary of being immersed in obscenity. In 1973, in *Miller v. California*,[18] the Supreme Court is clearly wanting to shake the obscenity monkey off its back. In this case, the Court attempted to set obscenity standards that state legislatures could use in drafting legislation so the state courts could decide obscenity cases.

In *Miller*, the Court said that it had "recognized that the States have a legitimate interest in prohibiting dissemination or exhibition of obscene material when the mode of dissemination carries with it a significant danger of offending the sensibilities of unwilling recipients or of exposure to juveniles."[19] It is within this context of a legitimate state interest in prohibiting that kind of dissemination, the Court says, that it is setting the standard for determining what material is obscene. The Court also flatly stated what the standard is not: It rejected the *Fanny Hill* approach, which required prosecutors to prove that material was "utterly without redeeming social value," thus requiring them to "prove a negative," which is "virtually impossible." The *Fanny Hill* test was "unworkable," and, according to the Court, not a single Justice still supported that test.[20] While repeating its view that "obscene material is unprotected by the First Amendment," the Court added that it is always dangerous for states to try to regulate expression. Thus the Court limited the "permissible scope" of regulation to works that "depict or describe sexual conduct."[21]

The Court in *Miller* set these "basic guidelines" for determining obscenity:

(a) whether "the average person, applying contemporary community standards" would find that the work, taken as a whole, appeals to the prurient interest, (b) whether the work depicts or describes, in a patently offensive way, sexual conduct specifically defined by the applicable state law, and (c) whether the work, taken as a whole, lacks serious literary, artistic, political, or scientific value.

The Court also decided it needed to give a little further explanation of section b, which relates to whether the work depicts sexual conduct in a "patently offensive way." It said that under that section, a state legislature could include: "(a) Patently offensive representations or descriptions of ultimate sexual acts, normal or perverted, actual or simulated. (b) Patently offensive representation or descriptions of masturbation, excretory functions and lewd exhibition of the genitals."[22]

The Court thought that if those guidelines were followed by the states when they wrote their obscenity statues, then First Amendment rights would be adequately protected by appellate courts doing an independent review of any constitutional claims.[23] And as a final effort in getting the monkey of obscenity cases off its back, the Court said there was no "national 'community standard'" of what appeals to "prurient interest" or is "patently offensive": "Our nation is simply too big and too diverse for this Court to reasonably expect that such standards could be articulated for all 50 States in a single formulation."[24]

After deciding *Miller* in 1973, the Supreme Court felt fairly satisfied that now, under state statutes, only materials depicting "hard core" sexual conduct would be subject to prosecution, and that state appellate courts could adequately review constitutional attacks on convictions. The Supreme Court also felt fairly satisfied that "fair notice" would be given to dealers in that kind of material.[25]

But in 1974, the Court was back in the obscenity business in a case involving a film by Mike Nichols, *Carnal Knowledge*. In *Jenkins v. Georgia*, 418 U.S. 153 (1974), the Court unanimously overturned the conviction of the manager of a Georgia theater who was fined $750 and sentenced to a year in jail for distributing "obscene material." The Georgia Supreme Court had upheld the conviction.

In 1987, the Supreme Court, in *Pope v. Illinois*,[26] made a ruling concerning the third leg of the *Miller v. California* test for obscenity—the question of "whether the work, taken as a whole, lacks serious literary, artistic, political or scientific value." The Court said that this part of the *Miller* test is to be determined by a "reasonable person" standard, and not an "average person" standard. Perhaps a "reasonable person" would be more lenient than an "average person" in some locales; of course, the implication is that the "average person" in some locales is unreasonable about the topic of obscenity.

Obscenity law protects rockers and rappers—and everyone else.

APPENDIX: OBSCENITY

BRIEF HISTORY OF LEGAL TESTS FOR OBSCENITY

Hicklin Test

From the 1868 English case of *Regina v. Hicklin*:
> Whether the tendency of the material is to corrupt minds that are "open to such immoral influences."

Judge Woolsey's Test

From the 1933 case about James Joyce's book, *Ulysses*, in a New York Federal District Court:

a. Determine whether the author's intent is "pornographic" or literary by looking at the book as a whole.
b. Determine the book's dominant effect on normal, reasonable people, not on children or abnormal adults.

Roth Test

In 1957, the U.S. Supreme Court rejected the *Hicklin* test, and a majority of five justices agreed to this new test:
> "Whether to the average person, applying contemporary community standards, the dominant theme of the material taken as a whole appeals to prurient interest."

Fanny Hill Test

In 1966, a three-Justice plurality of the U.S. Supreme Court said three elements must be present before a work can be considered obscene:

a. "the dominant theme of the materials taken as a whole appeals to a prurient interest";
b. "the material is patently offensive because it affronts contemporary community standards relating to the description or representation of sexual matters"; and
c. "the material is utterly without redeeming social value."

Miller v. California Test

In 1973, the United States Supreme Court said the "basic guidelines" for determining obscenity are:

a. "whether 'the average person, applying contemporary community standards' would find that the work, taken as a whole, appeals to the prurient interest";

b. "whether the work depicts or describes, in a patently offensive way, sexual conduct specifically defined by the applicable state law"; and
c. "whether the work, taken as a whole, lacks serious literary, artistic, political, or scientific value."

Under section b, a state legislature could include:

1. "patently offensive representations or descriptions of ultimate sexual acts, normal or perverted, actual or simulated"; and
2. "patently offensive representations or descriptions of masturbation, excretory functions and lewd exhibition of the genitals."

The Court in *Miller* said there was no "national 'community standard'" of what appeals to "prurient interest" or is "patently offensive." In 1987, in *Pope v. Illinois*, the Court said a "reasonable person" standard, not a "community" standard, should be applied to determine whether a work lacks "serious . . . value."

APPENDIX: FEDERAL STATUTES RELATING TO OBSCENITY

All 50 states have obscenity statutes. These statutes, of course, must follow the guidelines established in *Miller v. California*, discussed earlier.

The following statutes comprise the federal law on obscenity.

SELECTED OBSCENITY STATUTES

Title 18 United States Code

§ 1465. Transportation of obscene matters for sale or distribution

Whoever knowingly transports in interstate or foreign commerce for the purpose of sale or distribution, or knowingly travels in interstate commerce, or uses a facility or means of interstate commerce for the purpose of transporting obscene material in interstate or foreign commerce, any obscene, lewd, lascivious, or filthy book, pamphlet, picture, film, paper, letter, writing, print, silhouette, drawing, figure, image, cast, phonograph recording, electrical transcription or other article capable of producing sound or any other matter of indecent or immoral character, shall be fined not more than $5,000 or imprisoned not more than five years, or both.

The transportation as aforesaid of two or more copies of any publication or two or more of any article of the character described above, or a combined total of five such publications and articles, shall create a presumption that such publications or articles are intended for sale or distribution, but such presumption shall be rebuttable.

§ 1466. Engaging in the business of selling or transferring obscene matter

(a) Whoever is engaged in the business of selling or transferring obscene matter, who knowingly receives or possesses with intent to distribute any obscene book, magazine, picture, paper, film, videotape, or phonograph or other audio recording, which has been shipped or transported in interstate or foreign commerce, shall be punished by imprisonment for not more than five years or by a fine under this title, or both.

(b) As used in this section, the term "engaged in the business" means that the person who sells or transfers or offers to sell or transfer obscene matter devotes time, attention, or labor to such activities, as a regular course of trade or business, with the objective of earning a profit, although it is not necessary that the person make a profit or that the selling or transferring or offering to sell or transfer such material be the person's sole or principal business or source of income. The offering for sale of or to transfer, at one time, two or more copies of any obscene publication, or two or more of any obscene article, or a combined total of five or more such publications and articles, shall create a rebuttable presumption that the person so offering them is "engaged in the business" as defined in this subsection.

§ 1467. Criminal forfeiture

(a) Property subject to criminal forfeiture. A person who is convicted of an offense involving obscene material under this chapter . . . shall forfeit to the United States such person's interest in—

(1) any obscene material produced, transported, mailed, shipped, or received in violation of this chapter . . .

(2) any property, real or personal, constituting or traceable to gross profits or other proceeds obtained from such offense; and

(3) any property, real or personal, used or intended to be used to commit or to promote the commission of such offense, if the court in its discretion so determines, taking into consideration the nature, scope, and proportionality of the use of the property in the offense.

NOTES

1. *Jacobelis v. Ohio*, 378 U.S. 184, 197 (1964) (Justice Harlan, concurring).

2. *Interstate Circuit, Inc. v. Dallas*, 390 U.S. 676, 704 (1968) (Justice Harlan, dissenting in part).

3. *Miller v. California*, 413 U.S. 15, 22 (1973).

4. See 18 U.S.C. 1461 (reprinted in Appendix: Federal Statutes Relating to Obscenity).

5. L.R. 3 Q.B. 360 (1868).

6. *United States v. One Booke Called "Ulysses,"* 5 F Supp. 182, 183 (S.D.N.Y. 1933).

7. *Roth v. United States*, 354 U.S. 476 (1957).

8. Ibid. at 487–489.

9. Ibid. at 481–485.

10. Ibid. at 491–494.

11. *Memoirs v. Massachusetts*, 383 U.S. 413 (1966).

12. In a plurality decision there is no majority agreement; the highest number of agreeing views wins. In this case, the number was three.

13. *Paris Adult Theatre I v. Slaton*, 413 U.S. 49, 73 (1973) (Brennan, dissenting).

14. See *Miller v. California*, 413 U.S. 15, 22 (1973).

15. *Redrup v. New York*, 386 U.S. 767 (1967).

16. This "practice of summarily reversing convictions" occurred in 31 cases. See *Miller v. California*, 413 U.S. 15, 22 n.3 (1973).

17. *Cohen v. California*, 403 U.S. 15, 25 (1971).

18. *Miller v. California*, 413 U.S. 15 (1973).

19. Ibid. at 18 (citing, among other cases, *Stanley v. Georgia*, 394 U.S. 557, 567 [1969]).

20. Ibid. at 24–25.

21. Ibid. at 23–24.

22. Ibid. at 24–25.

23. Ibid.

24. Ibid. at 30–34.

25. Only dealers were subject to prosecution because the Court had already held in a previous case that the First Amendment prohibits "making mere private possession of obscene material a crime." See *Stanley v. Georgia*, 394 U.S. 557 (1969). But in *Osborne v. Ohio*, 495 U.S. 103 (1990), covered *infra*, the Court decided that mere possession of pornography using children—"kiddie porn"—could be outlawed.

26. *Pope v. Illinois*, 481 U.S. 497 (1987).

7

"Let's Spend the Night Together," Uhhh, "Some Time Together," Making Rock Acceptable: "The Ed Sullivan Show"

Stephen H. Wheeler

"The Ed Sullivan Show" of the 1950s and 1960s could launch a career and sell records, and Ed Sullivan could make or break a performer. Jackie Mason found himself unable to obtain future bookings after October 18, 1964, because of what Sullivan perceived to be an obscene gesture directed toward him as Mason finished his comedy routine. As far as Sullivan was concerned, Mason would never appear on *his* show again. Sullivan later recanted his decision, but Mason's career was damaged.[1] However, it was the introduction of new acts that allowed Sullivan's show to influence the country's popular culture. This chapter will explain how.

The Sullivan show became ingrained into American popular culture through its enormous popularity. Going from the thirteenth overall top-rated show in the 1950s and the fifth overall top-rated show in the 1960s, "The Ed Sullivan Show" garnered a sizeable segment of the American viewing public when they turned their television dials to CBS on Sunday evenings.[2] Paul M. Hirsch adroitly recounted that top-rated program such as "The Ed Sullivan Show" became part of popular culture because it could "cut across demographic boundaries and present to diverse groups of Americans a set of common symbols, vocabularies, information, and shared experiences."[3]

In his attempts to appeal to such a diverse audience, Sullivan may have subconsciously defined and reinforced those common cultural values that middle-class and upper-class Americans thought acceptable. One such cultural value concerned rock 'n' roll. With few exceptions, Sullivan showcased rock performers or groups who would be inoffensive. When he "requested" in January 1967 that the Rolling Stones change their lyrics of "Let's Spend the Night Together" to "Let's Spend Some Time Together," Sullivan was more than just cognizant of CBS censors. He sanitized.

Mick Jagger, lead singer for the Rolling Stones, who in February 1967, would be arrested on drug possession charges in Britain along with band member Keith

Richards, said he "sang mumble," rather than kowtow to censors about the lyrics of "Let's Spend the Night Together."[4] The Rolling Stones were infamous for pushing to the civilized edge in their private lives and their music. "In their music, the Stones pioneered British rock's tone of ironic detachment and wrote about offhand brutality, sex as power, and other taboos. Mick Jagger was branded a 'Lucifer' figure, thanks to songs like 'Sympathy for the Devil.'"[5]

Sullivan felt he had to become a buffer and a censor with groups like the Stones. He could not afford to alienate his primary adult audience by bringing into their living rooms someone who under the best of situations would never have made it through the front door. However, whether television actually sided with the development and hence acceptability of rock music is open to question. Joe Stuessy argues, "Generally television has not been a major factor in the development of rock."[6] Going even further in downplaying the role of television vis-a-vis rock 'n' roll, Jim Curtis maintains, "Despite the epochal appearances of Elvis and the Beatles on 'The Ed Sullivan Show' . . . television did not play a significant role in the development of rock 'n' roll until MTV."[7] Among those who have argued that television served as a significant medium through which rock music was enhanced, Peter Wicke writes that the reason rock music spread so rapidly was because it was "the first form of music whose development was linked to radio, film, and *television*."[8] (Emphasis added.)

Given this dichotomy, it is valid to explore if television actually played a significant role in the acceptability of rock music and if so, how. It is the contention here that popular variety show's, such as "The Ed Sullivan Show," waylaid fears and demonstrated to mainstream American adults that rock 'n' roll was not the harbinger of the nation's possible downfall of its youth.

Television grew so rapidly after World War II that by 1953, two-thirds of all American homes had a little gray screen.[9] Television contributed to the demise of network radio and caused an unforeseen impact on the programming of popular music. As more and more network programs vacated radio for television, radio programmers searched to fill the void. Initially, what they found was rhythm and blues.

When live, network radio shows dominated the airwaves in the 1930s and 1940s, black music was summarily cut off the radio.[10] But television, by the 1950s, absorbed those network radio shows, and opened the door for black records to be aired on radio. Coupled with post–World War II social changes, such as the civil rights movement, "a change was gonna come" to American popular music as more and more white teenagers became familiar with rhythm and blues.

David Szatmary credited Alan Freed as being responsible for this "revolution." He writes that Freed, who had been hired in 1951 to play classical music for WJW in Cleveland, "witnessed the reaction of white teenagers to R&B as the music blared in a local record store."[11] Freed convinced his station manager to allow him to follow the classical program with a rock 'n' roll show. Picking as his theme song "Blues for Moondog," Freed named his show "The Moon Dog Rock 'n' Roll House Party." He worked tirelessly to promote the new music, organizing sold-out concerts such as the Moon Dog Coronation Ball for which he sold 18,000 tickets for a 9,000-seat auditorium. Freed became a popular radio personality, and in 1954, moved his show to WINS, New York, where he introduced thousands more to black music. His appearance in such films as *Don't Knock the Rock*, *Rock, Rock, Rock* and *Rock Around the Clock* further familiarized white youths with a musical format Freed had dubbed "rock 'n' roll."[12]

Opposition to the "new" music formed just as rapidly. Adults responded to supposedly obscene content or double entendre, in such songs as "Sixty-Minute Man" or "Work With Me Annie." Station officials feared a public outcry and many albums collected dust on station shelves. Rock music engendered additional criticism because of its appeal to white and black youths, it helped promote integration. The White Citizens Council of Birmingham, Alabama, contended that rock music, "'the basic, heavy-beat music of the Negroes,' appealed to 'the base in man, brings out animalism and vulgarity' and, most important, formed a 'plot to mongrelize America.'"[13]

Not only did rock music appear to undermine traditional sexual mores and race relations, especially in the South, but the larger record companies were also threatened by the new music. Because the newer independent labels "held a virtual monopoly on rock acts by 1955,"[14] record company executives needed a way to recapture the white teen market. Frank Sinatra would not work.

One solution was to "cover" the songs of black artists. Pat Boone copied Fats Domino's "Ain't that a Shame," which reached number two on the Billboard charts, and Little Richard's "Tutti Fruitti," which did not.[15] Boone's inane "covers" could have easily sounded the death knell of rock 'n' roll. At the same time, early television did little to advance rock music. Perhaps the closest that TV came was with the show "Your Hit Parade." Each week, the show's regular cast would perform live covers of the previous week's Top Ten songs. However, the "Your Hit Parade's" adult viewing audience lost interest and dwindled because of the increasing number of rock songs. Teen audiences also turned away because they "were not interested in Snooky Lanson's version of 'Hound Dog.'"[16] Given this dual rejection, the demise of "Your Hit Parade" is not surprising. What is astonishing is the "the Good Housekeeping seal of approval" provided for rock music by "The Ed Sullivan Show."

"The Ed Sullivan Show" began in June 1948 and continued for the next 23 years, with one man dominating Sunday night television viewing. This "performer" could not dance, sing, play a musical instrument, juggle plates, or even smile at times, yet he thoroughly and regularly entertained 50 million Americans.[17] Ed Sullivan became the toast of the town for several reasons. As a showman, Sullivan had an innate ability to know what would go over well with the home viewer.[18] At his best, Sullivan presented the ideal acts at the critical moment—the moment when America had heard enough about the newcomers to be monumentally curious, but somehow had missed (or had put off) seeing them previously.[19]

Perhaps most importantly with the show, according to Timothy Scheurer, "class distinctions broke down as audiences watched," revealing "all characteristics of the diversity of what we know as America."[20] In other words, Ed Sullivan provided a looking glass for Americans to see into, and to reflect their own values. Sullivan's variety-style format was a smorgasbord, designed to appeal to a generational cross-section of America. The more culturally refined were offered opera, the middle-class was provided with the likes of Louis Armstrong, blue-collar America was treated to vaudeville-type entertainment, teens were given their rock 'n' roll, and children got their Topo Gigio. While one segment of society eagerly waited for "their" moment, they watched what appealed to another segment. In this manner, Sullivan made "acceptable" programming, which one group may have previously refused.

Sullivan's first venture into providing his viewers with "current popular music" was not, as might be expected, the much-heralded appearance of Elvis Presley. In late 1955, Sullivan decided to give his audience "a taste" of rhythm and blues staged in a less threatening environment, their own living rooms. He hired Tommy "Dr. Jive" Smalls to present a 15-minute segment of the type of shows he had been doing in Harlem. Part of Dr. Jive's entertainment package included Bo Diddley. The Dr. Jive portion came off well, except for one hitch: Sullivan's producer wanted Diddley to sing the fastest rising song in the country, "Sixteen Tons." Bo informed the producer that he did not know "Sixteen Tons." To overcome this small difficulty, the producers and some members of the orchestra went over the song with him; then, deciding to leave nothing to chance, they wrote down the words in big letters on cue cards. When Bo Diddley was introduced, he strolled on stage and promptly performed "Bo Diddley." Coming offstage, he was met by the production staff, incredulous that he had not performed "Sixteen Tons." As a defense he offered, "Man, maybe that was 'Sixteen Tons' on those cards, but all I saw was 'Bo Diddley!'"[21]

If Sullivan was eager to promote Dr. Jive's rhythm and blues, he was less than enthusiastic about booking Elvis Presley—at least initially. When Sullivan was offered a Presley booking, he declined, claiming that Presley was unknown outside of the South. Sullivan based his decision reports of Elvis' overt sexuality; he *"wouldn't consider presenting Presley before a family audience."*[22]

However, after Presley appeared on the competitive "Steve Allen Show" and trounced Sullivan's ratings, Sullivan had a change of heart. He booked the singer for three shows. Even so, Sullivan remained mindful of his main audiences' sensibilities. While the first two performances provided the viewing audience with full views of Elvis, the public outcry over Presley's gyrations caused Sullivan to change the camera shots for the third appearance. According to David Szatmary, "Fearing a backlash from his usual viewers, the television host ordered that Elvis be filmed from the waist up, allowing the teenage audience to imagine the pelvic gyrations that took place off screen."[23]

While teenagers watching could only try to visualize Elvis' movements, adults would be spared having to see them and having their worst fears confirmed. To further assure his viewers that they were not witnessing the decline and fall of American civilization, Sullivan said for the benefit of all, "I want to say to Elvis and the country that this is a real decent, fine boy. We want to say that we've never had a pleasanter experience on our show with a big name than we've had with you. You're thoroughly all right."[24]

Presley's appearances on Sullivan, "attracted nearly 54 million viewers, or almost 83 percent of the television audience,"[25] and cracked the Ed Sullivan door to rock music, though not quite all the way. When record sales of Jerry Lee Lewis' "Whole Lotta Shakin" slowed as a result of radio stations refusing to play a too provocative song, Sun records attempted to book Lewis on the Sullivan show. Ever mindful of his target audience, Sullivan refused, saying, "that after Presley, he didn't want 'any more of that crap.'"[26]

Throughout the rest of the 1950s, Ed Sullivan continued to offer less-than-threatening rock performers, ranging from the Platters to the Everly Brothers to Frankie Lymon and the Teenagers. Always sandwiched between variety acts that appealed to an older audience, Sullivan inadvertently demonstrated to adults that the music their children were listening to was not as threatening as they believed. The fact that rock performers boosted Sullivan's ratings was not overlooked by other television shows.

Following the Elvis Presley appearance in 1956, several sitcoms such as "Ozzie and Harriet" and "The Donna Reed Show" began offering rock music to boost their own ratings. Not only did the ratings increase, but according to Richard Aquila, "The new music benefited from this exposure. The publicity boosted record sales and polished rock 'n' roll's image. As young and old viewers alike watched Ricky Nelson and other clean-cut teenagers singing in their living rooms, they became convinced that rock 'n' roll was not that bad after all."[27]

As a result of Sullivan's efforts, American viewers were able to see rock music as a nonthreatening, cross-gender phenomena. While he presented such female rock singers as Connie Francis and Lesley Gore, dressed in formal evening wear and hence less visually threatening, he was "said to be 'a staunch enemy of the tougher girl groups,' which presumably would have been the Shangri-Las and the Ronettes."[28] When the Supremes appeared on the Sullivan show, they, too, had performed wearing evening gowns for almost of all of their 15 performances. The one significant departure occurred when they introduced "Love Child" to Sullivan's audience. For this appearance, they discarded their glamorous outfits in favor of a look that was in keeping with the lyrics of the song: sweatshirts, cut-offs, and bare feet.[29] What is most significant about this particular episode is not that the song reached number one on the Billboard chart after its introduction on Sullivan; rather it is that Sullivan felt his adult viewers would not be turned off by the lyrical content of this song, or by the Supremes' new look. The Supremes had become acceptable to mainstream America and their lyrics were actually advancing a socially respectable embraced by mainstream America—chastity.

In late 1963, Sullivan sensed another musical phenomena about to burst on the scene, the Beatles. Not to be a johnny-come-lately again, as with the Elvis appearance, Sullivan booked the English foursome in February 1964. That performance provided Sullivan with his largest viewing audience ever, nearly 74 million. However, an appearance on the Sullivan show initially could not quiet criticism of the Beatles. William F. Buckley, Jr. warned his readers "that they weren't 'merely awful': 'They are so unbelievably horrible.'" Congressman James Tustin of California said "the Beatles and other rock musicians 'use Pavlovian techniques to provoke neurosis in their listeners.'"[30] Had Sullivan miscalculated viewer sensibilities by showcasing the Beatles? Not hardly. He overcame those criticisms and assuaged viewer concerns because of several factors. He had the Beatles on his show 10 times, although not always live. Through sheer repetition, adult viewers came to perceive the Beatles as less threatening. Too, Sullivan continued to receive favorable endorsements from television-watchdog groups. The National Association for Better Radio and Television recommended "The Ed Sullivan Show" for family viewing because of what it considered top quality, diversified entertainment. This same group found the Roy Rogers show objectionable for its "combination of murder, dull-witted reactions to story situations and unacceptable philosophy."[31] After the Beatles, the floodgates opened; rock became a regular feature on television throughout the 1960s.

Capitalizing on the popularity of rock, specialized shows such as "Shindig" and "Hullabaloo" won a teen following. With these shows, teens now had their own programs and did not have to sit through entertainment targeted for their parents before seeing acts intended for them.[32] The implication was clear: if Sullivan was going to retain the post-Beatle teen audience, he must continue to book major rock groups and at the same time do so in such a manner that they seemed almost matter-of-fact. He almost succeeded.

When the Rolling Stones first appeared on his show in 1964, Sullivan was so taken aback by the commotion their fans caused and the "freaky" appearance of the group that he tried to distance himself from the situation as much as possible. He even issued a statement claiming he had not been responsible for booking them and they would never again be on his program. In fact, "Sullivan had become so uptight that he contemplated never booking any more rock acts, and even banning teenagers from the theater."[33] What Sullivan wanted were groups that presented the clean, wholesome look of the "Dave Clark Five," who would appear 12 times.

Within a year of his "no Rolling Stone" edict, Sullivan ate his words. The Stones popularity had increased, and Sullivan recognized his own ratings would soar if they reappeared. Sullivan made them tidy up their appearance a bit. By having them back on the show, he was subtly assuring his mainstream audience that the Stones "were not really all that bad, and you might even allow your daughter to go out with one,"[34] Martin and Segrave wrote.

Sullivan's other fall from mainstream grace occurred in 1967; the culprits were the Doors. After the morning rehearsal, the production staff informed the group that the word "higher" was unacceptable for family viewing because of its drug overtones. After vaguely promising not to include the offensive word, the Doors performed. Surprisingly, Jim Morrison "forgot" to omit the offending word, and Sullivan told the group they would never appear on the Sullivan Show again. Values triumphed over popularity.

Nonetheless, Sullivan viewers were treated to a steady barrage of rock music from 1964 until the end of the decade. While Sullivan showcased popular groups, they still had to be nonthreatening in their appearance or in the content of their music. Thus, mainstream audiences were exposed to groups such as Herman's Hermits, Freddie and the Dreamers, Gerry and the Pacemakers, Peter and Gordon, and the Four Tops. Jefferson Airplane, rather than frighten adults with the implications of their song "White Rabbit," sang the less-threatening, "Crown of Creation."[35] Similarly, Sullivan did not have The Who sing their anthem of the teen generation, "My Generation," which adults might have found unnerving.

By the end of the 1960s, American television viewers, anesthetized by an innocuous and steady diet of rock music on "The Ed Sullivan Show," came to view rock 'n' roll as just another form of entertainment. With Sullivan's success, some 20 variety shows imitated his format. Faced with overwhelming competition, Sullivan and his show went off the air in 1971. But "The Ed Sullivan Show" has been a powerful force in the entertainment industry. For 23 years, Ed Sullivan, a cultural gatekeeper, helped define American popular culture; he pushed rock music into the mainstream by legitimizing its sounds, its looks, its beat, and its teenage audience.

NOTES

1. Michael Harris, *Always on Sunday. Ed Sullivan: An Inside View* (New York: Meredith Press, 1968), 165–167.

2. *The World Almanac and Book of Facts*, (New York: Scripps-Howard, 1991), 318.

3. Paul M. Hirsch, "The Role of Television and Popular Culture in Contemporary Society." In *Television: The Critical View*, 3rd edition, ed. by Horace Newcomb (New York: Oxford, 1982), 291.

4. Patricia Romanowski and Holly George-Warren, eds., *The New Rolling Stone Encyclopedia of Rock & Roll* (New York: Fireside, A Rolling Stone Press Book, 1995), 847.

5. Ibid., 845.

6. Joe Stuessy, *Rock and Roll: Its History and Stylistic Development* (Englewood Cliffs, NJ: Prentice-Hall, 1990), 367–368.

7. Jim Curtis, *Rock Eras: Interpretations of Music and Society, 1954–1984* (Bowling Green, OH: Bowling Green State University Press, 1987), 12.

8. Peter Wicke, *Rock Music: Culture, Aesthetics and Sociology* (Cambridge, MA: Cambridge University Press, 1987), 4.

9. Richard N. Current, et al., *American History: A Survey*, 8th edition (New York: McGraw-Hill, 1992), 863.

10. David P. Szatmary, *Rockin' in Time: A Social History of Rock and Roll*, 2nd edition (Englewood Cliffs, NJ: Prentice-Hall, 1991), 22.

11. Ibid., 22.

12. Ibid.

13. Ibid., 24.

14. Ibid., 27.

15. Fred Bronson, *The Billboard Book of Number One Hits* (New York: Billboard Publications, 1985), 2.

16. Stuessy, *Rock and Roll*, 78.

17. John Leonard, *A Really Big Show: A Visual History of "The Ed Sullivan Show."* Claudia Falkenburg and Andrew Solt, eds. (New York: Penguin, 1992), 23.

18. Fred and Stan Goldstein, *Prime Time Television: A Pictorial History from Milton Berle to Falcon Crest* (New York: Crown, 1983), 11.

19. Donna McCrohan, *Prime Time, Our Time: America's Life and Times Through the Prism of Television* (Rocklin, CA: Prima, 1990), 85.

20. Timothy Scheurer, "The Variety Show in TV Genres." In *TV Genres: A Handbook and Reference Guide*, Brian Rose, ed. (Westport, CT: Greenwood Press, 1985), 318.

21. Ed Ward, Geoffrey Stokes, and Ken Tucker, *Rock of Ages: The Rolling Stone History of Rock & Roll* (New York: Summit Books, 1986), 111.

22. Linda Martin and Kerry Segrave, *Anti-Rock: The Opposition to Rock 'n' Roll* (Hamden, CT: Archon Books, 1988), 63–64.

23. Szatmary, *Rockin' in Time*, 50.

24. Falkenburg and Solt, *A Really Big Show*, 188.

25. Szatmary, *Rockin' in Time*, 50.

26. Martin and Segrave, *Anti-Rock*, 75.

27. Richard Aquila, *The Old Time Rock and Roll: A Chronicle of an Era 1954–1963* (New York: Schirmer Books, 1989), 9.

28. Martin and Segrave, *Anti-Rock*, 104.

29. Bronson, *The Billboard Book*, 248.

30. Falkenburg and Solt, *A Really Big Show*, 196; and Ralph J. Gleason, "A Cultural Revolution." In *The Sounds of Social Change; Studies in Popular Culture*, ed. by R. Serge Denisoff and Richard A. Peterson (Chicago: Rand McNally, 1972), 138.

31. Frank Orme, *Television for the Family* (Los Angeles: National Association for Better Radio and Television, 1966), 59, 64.

32. Scheurer, "The Variety Show in TV Genres," 321.

33. Martin and Segrave, *Anti-Rock*, 146.

34. Ibid., 146–147.

35. Falkenburg and Solt, *A Really Big Show*, 217.

8

Rolling Stone's Response to Attempted Censorship of Rock 'n' Roll

Lindsey R. Fore

Rock 'n' roll music, touted by scholars and critics as "the first unavoidable mass cultural commodity explicitly aimed at teenagers,"[1] also has been labeled an "immense homogenizer that absorbs the musical traditions and innovations of people separated in every other way, by race, by economic class, by region, by ideology, and recycles them in endless combinations."[2] Regarded as "much more than music for its devotees; it is a subculture in the strictest sense of the word."[3] Initially, the majority of the writing on rock music took the position that rock music was a "low-grade gimmick,"[4] but later scholars of popular culture wrote on the social, economic, and political functions, and the music's possible implications. One ignored area has been censorship—the regulation or control of rock music. Because the acts of regulation or control influence not only individual expressions of rock—the artists' songs and stage performances—but the field of rock 'n' roll as a whole, researchers still need to examine the critical climate of the attempted control and regulation of rock music[5] from the inception of the music form through its development over the past 40 years. Thus, this chapter focuses on a decade-by-decade description of responses from the most popular, music-oriented mass media, such as *Variety* and *Billboard*, about those regulations and controls but in particular the major rock music magazine, *Rolling Stone*. Because *Rolling Stone* started publication 13 years after rock 'n' roll began, other magazines that specialized in popular music also will be used initially.

One attempted area of control of the new creative music sounds and messages is by public criticism. Public disapproval has been especially notable in the past decade by special interest groups, which have focused on the music at congressional hearings and has asked for specific censorship actions. Radio and television stations, as well as regulatory agencies, have banned particular rock and more recently rap music. Magazines for rock music consumers and the industry, such as *Billboard* and *Rolling*

Stone have served as outlets for the voicing of opinions and responses to such censorship attempts. These periodicals respond to the criticisms and also provide information on the possible implications of popular music.

In 1954, the fans of older music forms were disturbed when rock 'n' roll began as a new form of music.[6] Having emerged from a convergence of previously established types of music—country and western, rhythm and blues, and pop—rock attracted new fans, the World War II generation, and older, did not know what to make of this new music, nor did they appear to understand it.[7] The audience's confusion about the sounds, along with the objectionable content, paved the way for the attempted regulation of the music. The beat was alien, as *Time* magazine commented in 1956:

Characteristics [of rock music are]: an unrelenting, shocking syncopation that sounds like a bull whip; a choleric saxophone honking mating-call sounds; an electric guitar turned up so loud that its sound shatters and splits; a vocal group that shudders and exercises violently to the beat while roughly chanting either a near-nonsense phrase or a moronic lyric in hillbilly idiom.[8]

Editors of *Rolling Stone* later summarized, "Rock 'n' roll has always been a frank and sometimes vulgar music, with plenty of things for its critics not to like."[9] Associated with the 1950s concern about juvenile delinquency, "the hoodlum element," and obscenity, rock 'n' roll's roots were considered "lower class" and associated with disruptive elements.[10] As an over-riding theme, the association with immorality was the justification for attempts to control and regulate the music during each decade of musical changes and the growing trends of rock music during the subsequent years.

THE FIRST YEARS

The earliest censorship efforts concerned the lyrics. Even prior to rock 'n' roll as early as 1950, an official attempt was made to ban the shipping and selling of "obscene disks" throughout the United States through interstate commerce regulation. *Billboard* noted that the courts ruled that records fell under the same provision as films and printed material.[11] Broadcasters were conscious of potential problems over risque lyrics and would self-censor to avoid possible trouble. In 1951, Dottie O'Brien's "Four or Five Times" and Dean Martin's "Wham Bam, Thank You Ma'am" were banned from airplay by Los Angeles radio stations. In 1953, Congress had before it a bill to regulate interstate shipment of obscene music, although it was not passed.[12] These incidents dealt with concerns that would later be applied to rock 'n' roll for the next four decades.

When rock 'n' roll swept across the nation's popular music charts in 1954 to 1956, critics referred to a possible Communist plot, along with risque lyrics and Elvis' "obscene" movements, as dangers to impressionable youth. The Roman Catholic Church urged a boycott of the music, while theater owners, radio station managers, and local sheriffs' offices attempted to ban the playing of particular rock tunes and acts. Just as their music was banned by a radio station in St. Paul, Bill Haley and His Comets were prohibited from performing in Jersey City, New Jersey.[13]

When televised variety programs featured music acts, anti-rock activists worried about the music presentation and decent lyrics. In 1956, the popular "Ed Sullivan Show" initially refused to televise Elvis because of his suggestive pelvic movements. *Billboard* called for "clean lyric contests."[14] Musical director of Mutual Broadcasting System Phil Lampkin summarized those early years, "We are eliminating only those rock 'n' roll tunes which are distorted, monotonous, noisy music and/or suggestive or borderline salacious lyrics."[15]

THE 1960s AND 1970s

At the beginning of the 1960s, the criticism and controls concerned the suggestive lyrics and presentation, but moved as did the country to political content and the artists' deviant lifestyles. The criticism was chilling and the censorship ultimate. Local broadcasters refused to air songs, and those artists deemed obscene or overtly violent by anti-rock advocates. "Tell Laura I Love Her," the story of a stock car driver, recorded by Ray Peterson in 1960, was called the "Death Disk" and even the BBC refused to play such "tasteless and vulgar" subject matter.[16] Teens in America and Great Britain still purchased the records.

Primarily concerned with the political and social aspects of American society, folk rock engendered a negative response that centered on the artists' ideologies about the war, civil rights, and sexuality embedded in the lyrics, and the musicians' lifestyles, which were associated with leftist organizations, drugs, alcohol, and sexual promiscuity. *Variety* wrote that the major complaints were about artists such as Joan Baez and Bob Dylan. In 1963, ABC-TV's music-oriented variety show, "Hootenanny," stopped Pete Seeger and The Weavers from appearing because of Seeger's past political affiliations.[17] That same year, CBS barred folk-singer Bob Dylan's performance of a song satirizing the John Birch Society on "The Ed Sullivan Show."[18]

Billboard pointed out that such highly political subject matter coincided with the beginning of the Vietnam War.[19] The rock musicians sang of the increasingly controversial war as well as protest and peace movements. As the country grew more divided over the war, the artists' song lyrics became more strident. *Variety* noted that the American military banned songs of the protest movement from being sent or played overseas on armed forces radio stations.[20] By the latter part of the 1960s, anti-rock advocates also went after those songs that referred to sexuality and drugs or dealt with the artists' personal lifestyles. By 1970, even the British BBC would not play groups such as the Beatles because of their references to drug use and sexual activities, according to *Variety*.[21]

The controversy over rock music in the 1970s centered around lifestyles: sex, drugs, and obscene language. Opening the decade was the performance of the musical *Hair*, which not only contained nudity in the theatrical performance but also explicit sexual subject matter in the soundtrack. The provocative play was held up for six weeks pending a court decision concerning free expression in music and theater.[22]

Also, the Federal Communications Commission (FCC) issued a warning to all broadcasters to "keep tabs on any recordings that might 'promote or glorify' illegal drugs." Although only a warning, many songs were cut from the airwaves.[23] The FCC also reacted with concern over the foul language and community standards in broadcasts. The FCC fined WUHY, an educational radio station in Philadelphia, when Grateful Dead singer Jerry Garcia used several profane words during an interview.[24] Before airing John Lennon's song "Working Class Hero," a majority of radio stations edited the song to exclude a profane word.[25]

Incidents of control in the 1970s followed the same pattern as the previous two decades. Michael Greene summarized the situation in *Billboard* magazine:

Rock has been under siege from the very first. In the '50s, the anti-rock brigade blamed the music for juvenile delinquency. In the '60s and '70s, drug abuse was the obsession, plus the fact that rock 'n' roll was allied with the anti-war movement. The excuses change but the [opposition] always has the same thing in mind—to make rock 'n' roll safe, to sanitize it for our protection.[26]

THE 1980s AND 1990s

The 1980s sparked a rapid increase in banning music. Organized groups such as the Parents' Music Resource Center (PMRC) formalized the movement that had begun with the inception of rock music (see Chapter 1). In addition to the previous concerns about lyrics referring to drug use, explicit sex, and the reactions of radio and television station managers, the PMRC wanted regulating devices such as record-rating and record-labeling. Senate hearings alerted the citizenry about the evils that lie within rock lyrics."[27] During the 1980s, artists were accused, even put on trial, for causing the suicides of several teens who listened to the "suicidal" heavy metal lyrics in the artists' music. The content of the lyrics is still at the heart of the concerns. Peggy Mann of the PMRC claimed that "today's rock music extols everything from rape, incest and homosexuality to sadomasochism and bestiality."[28]

From the late 1980s and into the 1990s, the PMRC, through media appeals and increased exposure on talk shows, in magazines and in newspapers, drew a following and began pressuring record companies to label albums with questionable lyrics.[29] By 1985, record companies labeled artists' records and tapes containing "offensive" lyrics. By the early 1990s, "in an effort to head off the proposed state laws, the companies agreed to use a standardized warning label.[30] One federal judge found 2-Live Crew's 1990 album *As Nasty as They Wanna Be* to be obscene. Artists such as Madonna, Red Hot Chili Peppers, Prince, and Ozzy Osbourne were the targets of "legal attacks claiming their performances were indecent or obscene."[31] Politicians such as Newt Gingrich and Bob Dole, Republican leaders in Congress, blamed music for the moral erosion of American society.

ROLLING STONE MAGAZINE

In 1967, *Rolling Stone* magazine began as an outlet for the growing trend of rock music news. The emphasis was not just on rock 'n' roll music, but the booming youth culture of the late 1960s and early 1970s, a culture that included such radical concepts as free love and "cultural bohemianism."[32] *Rolling Stone* founder Jann Wenner wrote in an open letter to the readers, the magazine "is not just about music but also the things and attitudes that the music embraces."[33] In the rock "revolution" climate, Wenner said as time went on he began to interpret that charter rather broadly. While the music was the generational glue, the ideas about youth—"personal relationships, social values, political ethics and the way we wanted to conduct our lives"—had been previously ignored by other media. The mainstream media, Wenner wrote, paid scant attention to the biggest stories of the times, "The emerging generational upheaval in America."[34] Beginning with only $8,000 and a staff composed primarily of volunteers, Wenner turned this small, biweekly magazine into a multi-million dollar publication with a circulation of more than one million. The format evolved to include more general entertainment and a broader array of political and social issues. Still, *Rolling Stone* focused on the music industry and leadership in reporting music news.

Even though rock music had been on the scene for 13 years, *Rolling Stone* quickly provided comprehensive reporting of music news and became highly influential among youth. As Chet Flippo wrote in *The History of Rolling Stone*, "it is impossible to overestimate the impact that it [*Rolling Stone*] had on young readers. As many have remarked, for the first time everything they wanted was assembled there for them: the music, the musicians, the new attitudes; all presented in a style that was both exuberant and believable."[35]

The first articles about attempts to control and regulate the music did not appear until 1969. Most were summaries of one page or less, the others were fairly substantial articles of three to six pages.[36] Only 14 articles written from 1969 through 1984 were found located under the headings "censorship in music," "popular music and politics," and "moral and religious aspects of rock music." All but one of these articles appeared in the first 20 pages of the magazine, indicating a prominent position in the publication.

The content of these 14 articles largely coincided with the then popular issues regarding the control of rock music. In 1970, such articles about song lyrics included "Christ They Know It Ain't Easy"[37] and "Lennon's Song: The Man Can't Fuck Our Music."[38] Other articles briefly covered regulatory agencies' control and tended to be more straight reporting of the status surrounding a particular event, or a "foe" of rock 'n' roll and its "satanic" influences, such as established religion, and the slow acceptance of "obscenity" or sexual explicity into rock music.

With the PMRC's mobilization by the mid-1980s, *Rolling Stone*'s coverage increased rapidly. This parent group, formed by the wives of Washington, D.C. politicians, and its influence appeared to cause the stampede. From 1985 to 1991, the magazine carried 26 articles on various aspects of control, an average of four per year. Twenty of those stories appeared in the first 25 pages of the magazine with seven longer pages, rather than the usual one-page summaries. *Rolling Stone* covered the various city ordinances aimed at obscenity at rock concerts, such as in San Francisco.[39]

Rolling Stone's major censorship topics concerned stickering, labeling, and ratings, in conjunction with the tracking of PMRC's efforts.[40] Items such as "CBS Sets Policy on Explicit Lyrics," appeared concerning proposed legislation to require record companies to label material containing explicit subject matter.[41] The magazine wrote about the Musicland chain as the only store to require IDs with the majority of items listed as rap recordings. Other articles covered the trials of Judas Priest concerning the effects of his lyrics on a teenager who committed suicide[42] and 2-Live Crew's obscenity.[43]

Rolling Stone's anti-censorship sentiments included blatant disdain for the PMRC's actions with an editorial placed in the middle of the article. Detailing the 1985 Senate hearings, *Rolling Stone* stated, "The Parents' Music Resource Center's proposal is unworkable and unnecessary and comes perilously close to censorship."[44] A three-page article, entitled "At a Loss for Words: Record Industry Acceptance of Stickering is Already Having a Chilling Effect,"[45] was clearly an anti-labeling opinion piece. *Rolling Stone* argued that control efforts have a negative effect on the industry: "The concessions [voluntary labeling] sound disturbingly like self-censorship. Who needs legislation if the record companies voluntarily slap labels on their albums and if record companies like Circles won't sell those albums to minors?"[46]

As another example, "To Sticker or Not to Sticker,"[47] describes the battle as "the nit-picking over lyrics" but admits, "Despite attempts to placate the opposition by hiring listeners and tagging albums as seemingly inoffensive as Andrew Ridgeley's 'Son of Albert,' record companies may be fighting a losing war."[48] *Rolling Stone*'s editorial bias can be exemplified by the kinds of stories the magazine covered. If the amount of articles are any kind of indication, not until the mid-1980s did the magazine appear to be concerned about negative reactions to the music and possible censorship through regulation and labeling. Perhaps for the first 17 or so years, the editors' lifestyles[49] may have caused them to ignore the creeping controls and attempts to regulate.

Since 1956, censorship, regulation, and control have been issues concerning rock 'n' roll. Public indignation and even the most virulent criticism were in response to the very nature of the music form. Rock music was so alien in the beginning that it lent itself to being scrutinized and "sanitized," at first over the sounds, then the lyrics.[50] Yet, rock continued, albeit in many hybrid forms. *Rolling Stone* comments that the music was "to dance on the outer edge of what society finds acceptable. It always has."[51] The 40 years of rock music and its offshoots indicate that the music flourished despite vehement opposition. This chapter is but a brief look at the changing decades of the controversies about rock 'n' roll and the attempted controls over the music as well as music publications' coverage of those issues. Even the more mainstream music magazines told of the controls and those who attempted to control.

Specialized media relay what is happening to a particular audience. Popular music magazines, such as *Billboard* and *Variety*, described the public response to rock music decade by decade. The *Rolling Stone*'s editorial stance covered not only the music and the mainstream response to it, but also lifestyles and attempted controls of the music and all that was connected to it.

NOTES

1. Simon Frith and Andrew Goodwin, eds., *On Record: Rock, Pop, and the Written Word* (New York: Pantheon Books, 1990), 2.

2. Podell, *Rock Music in America* (New York: The H.W. Wilson Co., 1987), 5.

3. Jonathan Eisen, *The Age of Rock* (New York: Random House, 1969), xi.

4. Frith and Goodwin, *On Record*, 2.

5. Horace Newcomb, *Television, the Critical View* (New York: Oxford University Press, 1987), 3-4.

6. See Carl Belz, *The Story of Rock* (New York: Oxford University Press, 1986) and Podell, *Rock Music in America*.

7. Belz, *The Story of Rock*.

8. "Yeh-Heh-Heh-Hes, Baby," *Time*, June 1956, 58.

9. "Rock Ratings," *Rolling Stone* (1985).

10. "Yeh-Heh-Heh-Hes, Baby," 58.

11. "U.S. Drive on Dirty Discs," *Billboard* (Feb. 1959), 14.

12. "Sked Early Action on Dirty Disk Law," *Billboard* (Feb. 1953), 30.

13. A. Portch, "Manager of Bill Haley Defends the 'Real Thing,'" *Melody Maker* (1956), 43.

14. "Charts Clean Lyrics Contest," *Billboard* (July 1958), 6,12.

15. J. Bundy, "Censored R & R on New MBS Disk Service Format," *Billboard* (Aug. 1958), 2.

16. "Blitz on 'Death' Record," *Melody Maker* (Oct. 1960), 13.

17. "Dick Clayton's 'Blacklist Festival,'" *Variety* (May 1963), 57.

18. "CBS (Ed Sullivan) Bans Folksinger Dylan for John Birch Satirization," *Variety* (May 1963), 2.

19. "ABC 'Blacklist' Stirs Folk People," *Billboard* (March 1963), 1,8.

20. "Bar 'Protest' Songs from Europe GI's," *Variety* (Aug. 1965), 1.

21. "Sex & Drugs Still Occasional Ban Victims of Funny Duddy BBC," *Variety* (July 1970), 39.

22. "Uncut 'Hair' Reopens in Boston, Saved by Supreme Court Ruling," *Variety* (May 1970), 57.

23. M. Hall, "FCC Clarification Note Shaky Bridge Over Troubled Water," *Billboard* (April 1971), 1,10.

24. Ben Fong-Torres, "When Humor Is No Longer Funny," *Rolling Stone* (July 1970), 8.

25. Ibid., 1,6.

26. Michael Greene, "Censorship May Be Just Around the Corner: Why Are These People Laughing?" *Billboard* (Aug. 1986), 40.

27. Joe Saltzman, "Porn Rock," *USA Today* (Jan. 1986), 91.

28. Peggy Mann, "How Shock Rock Harms Our Kids," *Readers' Digest* (July 1988), 101.

29. David Zucchino, "Big Brother Meets Twisted Sister," *Rolling Stone* (Nov. 1985), 9.

30. Michael Goldberg and Jeffrey Ressner, "Retailers Take on Stickering," *Rolling Stone* (April 1990), 26.

31. Stan Soocher, "2-Live Crew Take the Rap," *Rolling Stone* (Aug. 1990), 19.

32. Chet Flippo, *The History of Rolling Stone* (1974), 159.

33. Ibid., 163; and Jann S. Wenner, "Introduction." In *The Best of Rolling Stone, 25 Years of Journalism on the Edge*, Robert Love, ed. (New York: Doubleday, 1993), xi.

34. Ibid.

35. Ibid., 163.

36. Based on a thorough search of the *Reader's Guide to Periodical Literature*, *The Music Index*, and the Infotrac system.

37. Ben Fong-Torres, "When Humor Is No Longer Funny," 8.

38. Ben Fong-Torres, "Lennon Song: The Man Can't Fuck Our Music," *Rolling Stone* (Feb. 1970), 1,6.

39. Michael Goldberg, "Crackdown on 'Obscene' Shows: New San Francisco Law Aimed at Rock 'n' Roll Concerts," *Rolling Stone*, 466 (Jan. 30, 1986), 9.

40. Robert Love, "Washington Wives' Set Their Sights on Video," *Rolling Stone* (Oct. 1985), 18; G. Sandow, "Doctors Deny PMRC Alliance," *Rolling Stone* (Feb. 1990), 34.

41. Michael Goldberg, "CBS Sets Policy on Explicit Lyrics," *Rolling Stone* (April 1986), 13.

42. Michael Goldberg, "Heavy Metal on Trial," *Rolling Stone* (Dec. 1988), 15; Kim Neely, "Judas Priest Gets Off the Hook," *Rolling Stone* (Oct. 1990), 39.

43. Alan Light, "2-Live Crew Beats the Rap," *Rolling Stone* (Nov. 1990), 27.

44. "Rock Ratings," *Rolling Stone*, (1985).

45. Michael Goldberg, "At a Loss for Words: Record-Industry Acceptance of Stickering Is Already Having Chilling Effect," *Rolling Stone* (May 1990), 19–22.

46. Ibid., 19.

47. Jeffrey Ressner, "To Sticker or Not to Sticker," *Rolling Stone* (Feb. 1991), 17.

48. Ibid. See also Gerald Seligman, "Twelve States Consider 'Porn Rock' Legislation," *Rolling Stone* (June 1986), 19; Kim Neely, "Rockers Sound Off," *Rolling Stone* (Aug. 1990), 27–29; and Kim Neely, "Louisiana Law to Require LP Stickers," *Rolling Stone* (Aug. 1990), 35.

49. *New York Newsday*, 9 March 1995; and "The Secret Everyone Seems to Know," *Washington Post*, 9 March 1995.

50. Belz, *The Story of Rock*, 57.

51. "Rock Ratings," *Rolling Stone* (1985).

9

Deconstructing the Hip-Hop Hype: A Critical Analysis of the *New York Times'* Coverage of African-American Youth Culture

Patrick B. Hill

Just as America was basking in the afterglow of the crossover anthem, "We Are the World," black popular music culture of the mid-1980s, with its accompanying images of hybrid identity and utopian egalitarianism, underwent profound transformations. Indeed, the emergence of "rap hit this celebration of racial melding broadside." Since then, hip-hop culture, a formation in which rap music is only one element, not only has been a key influence on the tastes, styles, and modes of personal expression among American youth, but it also represented the emergence of a new cultural orthodoxy.[1]

Consequently, this unique, complex cultural formation has been greeted with considerable discussion and debate in the mass media. The *New York Times* has been a major forum for this often controversial public discourse. The *New York Times*, because of the esteem with which it is held by the most powerful segments of American society, serves as a cultural gatekeeper, agenda setter, and chief arbiter of news and information. For well over a century, the *Times* has held an important role in American public discourse about emerging cultural developments. The *Times* was selected for this study because of its close, physical proximity to those African-American communities in New York that gave birth to hip-hop culture.[2] The objective of this chapter is to critically survey the *New York Times'* coverage of hip-hop as it occurred within the social and political context of 1980s America.[3] Furthermore, this chapter seeks to compare its findings with those of an earlier study, which examined the content of the *Times'* coverage of Black popular music during the 1920s.[4]

The swirl of discussion and debate currently taking place over rap music is in many ways similar to mainstream responses to the emergence of jazz during the Prohibition era. Critics called the music "decadent," the "devil's music," and "jungle rhythm," according to John Frohnmayer, author of *Out of Tune, Listening to the First Amendment.*[5] Cities banned jazz performances as sinful. And in Chicago, no trumpet or saxophone playing was allowed after dark. The reaction was racist, as were turn-of-the-century prohibitions against ragtime, such as this 1899 railing:

A wave of vulgar, filthy and suggestive music has inundated the land . . . with its obscene posturing, its lewd gestures. Our children, our young men and women, are continually exposed . . . to the monotonous attrition of this vulgarizing music. It is artistically and morally depressing and should be suppressed by press and pulpit.[6]

As this Progressive era commentor suggests, the proper societal response was to first argue against such scandalous music, then attempt to stop it.

In the post-Cold War era, years free of the spectre of a "communist threat" and devoid of many clearly defined identities, clear distinctions separating "good" and "evil," "us" and "them," have become problematic. Consequently, without specific demons to mobilize popular consensus, national identities have become increasingly difficult to justify and maintain. Indeed, if the signifying practices of the mainstream media from 1985 to 1990 are any indication, many of these ominous figures were found in the inner cities of America.[7]

In January 1990, the *Washington Post* printed an editorial entitled "Hate, Rape and Rap" written by future second lady and record-labeling lobbyist Tipper Gore.[8] This article added to the considerable furor already taking place among policy makers (and their wives), civil libertarians, intellectuals, and concerned citizens about the emergence of rap music and hip-hop culture into the public sphere. The previous April, a young, white female investment banker was raped, brutally disfigured, and left for dead after jogging through New York City's Central Park. According to both news and police reports, the perpetrators were described as a "gang" of black teenagers out for a night of "wilding," which was a reference to "Wild Thing." The then popular tune by rap artist Tone Loc, was supposedly sung by the defendants in celebration of their alleged crime, after being detained by the New York Police Department.[9]

The misogynistic content of many rap lyrics including "Wild Thing," and the violent brutality of rape are rightfully causes for concern. However, contrary to the suggestion implicit in a litany of other examples, there is no necessarily casual relationship between rap music and violent crime. Nonetheless, hip-hop culture and African-American youth, especially males, have become associated in the mainstream media with not only rape, but the rise of drug trafficking, gang activity, carjacking, and violence against police.

Indeed, during a period in which the Soviet Union faded as a direct threat and in which explicitly race-based appeals are discouraged, the need to explain profound social ills prompted much of the mainstream media to use rap music metonymically to situate Black urban youth as convenient folk devils. Far from being simply dismissed as racist, conspiratorial or aberrant practices, the vilification of Black youth in mainstream media's initial efforts to comprehend rap music tells us much about how anxieties at the nexus of race, class and generational difference continue to animate the story world of American social relations.

Racial conflict has long been "the archetype of discord" within American society; the primordial conflict shaping all other social antagonisms, according to Howard Winant.[10] Moreover, as Cornel West points out, many Americans demonstrate a longstanding reluctance to engage in self-critique around this issue, except immediately after cataclysmic social upheavals like the Los Angeles rebellion. This reluctance, West wrote, contributes to a "political climate in which images, not ideas, dominate."[11]

Mainstream media practices within industrial societies assume a national cultural consensus. Implicit in this notion is the assumption that individuals within the nation share common frameworks of meaning and interpretation. Therefore, when events are "mapped" onto pre-existing cognitive frameworks, it is assumed that a diverse citizenry shall ultimately see themselves as a collective body despite differences of opinion.[12] This is thought to be especially true when the perceived interests of this constructed "we" are threatened by "otherness."

The ritual model of the communication process posits news as both a product and record of social reality. According to scholar James Carey, communication is "not being directed toward the extension of messages in space but the maintenance of society in time; not the act of imparting information, but the representation of shared beliefs."[13] News discourses, including hard news, editorial opinion, features, gossip, and even comics, endow the world with ideological and conceptual values from within the language and social dynamics of a culture. Thus, the examination of the *Times'* hip-hop coverage becomes a valuable way to understand how the core values of the culture are regulated and reaffirmed during a period of heightened class and race based antagonisms.

By centering research around the *New York Times'* coverage of hip-hop culture from 1985 to 1990, this study will examine all hip-hop and rap-related news and editorial items appearing in the *Times* Index as well as the National Newspaper Index.

Four distinct categories will be used for hip-hop news and editorial content: news themes, news type, news origination, and the main actors in the news. The news theme category will include issues related to violent events and rap's popular appeal, censorship/law, and business aspects, and the types of rap, such as gangsta rap, female rap, and progressive/radical rap. The news types will include hard news, features, editorials, letters to the editor, and concert/record reviews. The news origination category will include who originated the stories: staff reporters and writers, press services (AP, UPI, and Reuters), and article referents such as named sources and undetermined or unattributed sources used by the reporters. The main actor category will focus on hip-hop personalities who become the subject of the news.

After each of the articles was assigned to a subject category, then the story was rated either positive, negative, or neutral in tone. Though some subjectivity was required to code in this manner, this research used the content analysis guidelines developed by Bernard Berelson and Richard Budd to determine article direction. Negative depictions generally are those articles that reported social conflict, disorganization, or crime. Positive depictions are those reflecting social cohesion and cooperation among individuals or groups.[14] After analyzing and interpreting the 62 *Times'* articles and items published from 1985 to 1990, the information was compared with the findings of the Luther Williams' 1987 study of jazz coverage.

Three research questions form the basis of this study: What major changes took place in the reporting of hip-hop from 1985 to 1990? What were the dominant themes in these accounts? What viewpoints can be detected in the reports?

BACKGROUND

Hip-hop culture resonates in vastly different ways to the various communities and in particular New York City audiences. For its core audience, urban youth, hip-hop is a voice that uses the material and symbols of inner city life and death to articulate a search for meaning and empowerment. Thus, hip-hop transcends its aesthetic expression to function as an alternative media forum distinct from mainstream entities, such as the *New York Times*. In fact, Chuck D, leader of Public Enemy and a spokesman for hip-hop, often referred to rap music and the larger hip-hop formation as the "CNN of African-American youth." Controversial hip-hop performer Ice-T maintains that "rappers have been reporting from the front for years." Indeed, the weight of the available evidence supports Sister Souljah's claim that "whoever wants to speak to young people will have to come through the corridor of hip-hop."[15] Not unlike most mass media, hip-hop functions as social critic, agenda setter, commercial agent, cultural purveyor, catalyst for dissident press, as well as an outlaw.

This is not the first time that the *New York Times* and an emerging music culture has been studied. In 1987 Williams examined the *Times'* coverage of jazz from 1921 to 1929. Williams found a negative media response to jazz, which was often explicitly racist at the beginning of jazz popularity. However, when jazz began to enjoy an increasing measure of international acclaim, especially in Europe, the *Times'* coverage also changed. Toward the end of the 1920s, the *Times* both increased its jazz coverage and improved its tone. The *Times* also began to feature jazz personalities, although most often they were young white artists, such as Paul Whiteman or the Gershwin brothers. Williams points out that it was not until much later that the African-American originators of jazz were featured to any significant degree in the *Times*.[16]

Although the emergence of these two expressive genres are separated by sixty years, they share several parallels. Hip-hop emerged onto the popular consciousness during the 1980s at a stage of development similar to that which characterized jazz of the 1920s. Also, New York City was one of the most vibrant urban centers for both jazz and hip-hop. Though the proliferation of broadcast media has somewhat diminished newspaper dailies as popular sources of news and information over the years, the pre-eminence of the *New York Times'* news and cultural coverage makes it a medium worthy of study for novel cultural developments like hip-hop. In reconstructing the hostile climate of post-World War I America, the historical context responsible for early jazz, Williams characterizes the general nature of the *Times'* early coverage:

In 1921 readers of the *New York Times* were exposed to vehement assaults upon jazz by church and state. The clergy blamed jazz for a host of unseemly behaviors including fornication, suicide and alcohol abuse. In a pathetic combination of report and exaggeration, the *Times* printed that jazz had driven one musician to suicide.[17]

In the seven decades since then, the *New York Times* has, at least on the surface, benefited greatly from a more enlightened, professional, and "objective" editorial viewpoint relative to its coverage of African-American culture. Yet the argument of news coverage as society's mirror does not hold. Media scholar Gaye Tuchman points to the relationship between news organizations and the larger social structure they serve:

In their attitudes, in their organization, in their identifications of events as news, the news media are part and parcel of the society they serve. Although they claim to be merely a mirror to the world, that "mirror" might be better described as part of a reciprocal relationship between the news media and their environment. The news media are both "a cause" and "an effect."[18]

From 1985 to 1987, the first years of its reports on hip-hop, the *New York Times'* coverage could best be called sporadic. The *Times* had already begun to vilify hip-hop by associating it almost exclusively with incidents of violence and vandalism at concerts. For example, the *Times'* headlines were "On L.I., Fights Follow a Film on Rap Music" (6 November 1985); "42 Are Hurt as Gang Fighting Breaks Up California Concert" (19 August 1986); and "1 Killed, 5 Injured and 16 Arrested at Rap Concert" (26 November 1987). In addition, one *Times* news article, referring to Parents' Music Resource Center (PMRC), which Tipper Gore co-chaired, described rap music and hip-hop as negative influences by suggesting to its youthful listeners that "it's all right to beat people up."[19] Hard news of violence at rap concerts primarily made up the *Times'* early coverage. However, the *Times* did have features on personalities and the emergence of the art form onto the stage of mainstream popular culture.

As early as 1985, when there had been scant coverage overall, one *Times'* article acknowledged hip-hop's international appeal and its domestic crossover popularity and influence, similar to Williams' findings in his study on news coverage of jazz. For example, former rock critic turned hip-hop manager, Bill Adler commented:

Even in cities like Chicago, where no rap music is played on the radio, the [Run DMC] show attracted 15,000 people, which is some indication of rap's underground appeal . . . The rap industry now is a lot like Black rhythm and blues just before it was discovered by the mass audience in the 50s. The major radio programmers and record labels are trying to ignore that, but it's building a strong cross-racial audience anyway.[20]

Of the five years of coverage examined in this study, perhaps the least negative period for hip-hop in the *Times* appeared to be 1988. Though the coverage continued to be sparse, only six news items then, its general tenor was overwhelmingly more upbeat than what Williams found in the 1920s. In 1988, the *Times* acknowledged the multifaceted nature of hip-hop when music critic Glenn Collins wrote about hip-hop as a cultural complex consisting not only of "rap music" but also fashion, dance, language styles, and visual art.

Collins' article is unusual. Until its appearance, the dominant tendency in the *Times*' coverage ignored the range and diversity of hip-hop while focusing nearly exclusively on its most commercial component, rap music. Collins' article also included for the first time the input of scholars of African and African-American culture.[21]

The scholarly viewpoints of art historian and Yale University professor Robert Farris Thompson, black feminist writers Michele Wallace and bell hooks, and Harvard University professor Henry Louis Gates Jr. were the only academic specialists on African-American culture appearing in the *Times* throughout the study period. Moreover, the *Times* rarely sought out the opinions of activists or the academic leadership on hip-hop, or black music critics except for an occasional freelance contributor. The virtual absence of alternative viewpoints established by default the *Times*' indigenous staff of middle-class critics and reporters as the authorities on hip-hop. Acting as the experts on rap music to readership and advertisers, they dislocated rap music from the broader cultural field of hip-hop while largely ignoring the ways in which each are rooted in turn within the broader terrain of American culture.

Moreover, while acknowledging the contributions of individual African-American performers, the *Times* only once acknowledged hip-hop as an extension of earlier African-American culture. In a 1988 article entitled "Big Band Jazzmen and Rap Musicians: Soulmates," writer Peter Watrous compared the manner in which apparently dissimilar generations of African-American musicians fashioned new intertextual musical forms into existence through the clever yet eclectic use of music and other recorded material.[22] Though the issue of artistic property is implicit here, the *Times* coverage did not view it as central to the debates surrounding hip-hop as Williams found with the earlier writers in their coverage of jazz in the 1920s.[23]

By 1989, the *New York Times* extensive coverage of the hip-hop cultural phenomenon began in earnest.[24] The feature article, not spot news stories, became the primary vehicle through which items about hip-hop were published, except for controversies related to hip-hop personalities and concert-related violence. By 1989 and 1990, the largest body of hip-hop coverage appeared in the "Arts" section.

The *Times* focused more extensively on hip-hop when its music, dance and politics became increasingly familiar and popular among white suburban youth. The emergence of the popular group Public Enemy represented the personification of this trend. Though Public Enemy had both popular and critical acclaim beginning in 1987, it was during 1989 that the group's hip-hop classic, "Fight the Power," was featured in Spike Lee's film, *Do the Right Thing*. It was during 1989, after group member

Professor Griff's (Richard Griffin) widely publicized comments attributing "a majority of the wickedness" in the world to Jewish people, that the *Times* first took notice of the group. The second incident coincided with the December release of "Welcome to the Terrordome," which became another rap anthem. In the article, "Public Enemy, Loud and Angry, Is Far From Its Own Best Friend," *Times* music critic Jon Pareles wrote, "A band that has always insisted on the political impact of its music has become stubbornly, clumsily impolitic."[25]

The negative news construction of Public Enemy did not extend to other hip-hop acts. Even other overtly political performers such as KRS-One and hard core, gangsta rappers The Geto Boys and N.W.A. received far more positive coverage in the *Times*. However, none of these other hip-hop acts became associated with public utterances antagonistic to the *Times* or New York City's Jewish elites.[26]

As a result of the highly publicized controversies of 1989 and 1990 surrounding Public Enemy and 2-Live Crew, the general public was exposed not only to the ideological range within the rap community, but also the art form's emerging stylistic genres. In 1989, the *Times* began to report the increased expansion and diversification of hip-hop. Feature stories acknowledged the existence of West Coast "gangsta" rap, and "female rap." In 1990, the *Times* acknowledged in a feature entitled "Radical Rap: Of Pride and Prejudice" that hip-hop groups other than Public Enemy were articulating a militant message. According to writer Pareles, "Three years ago Public Enemy was the only group taking a combative stance on issues; now, half a dozen bands have followed up, while established groups make at least token efforts to be 'righteous'."[27]

There are striking discrepancies between the *Times'* response to "gangsta rap" and its representation of Public Enemy and "radical" rap. Made famous by Los Angeles groups N.W.A. and Ice-T, gangsta rap was greeted with alarm by various constituencies. Homosexual, feminist, and African-American communities protested against gangsta rap because of lyrical and thematic content glorifying gay bashing, misogyny, criminal violence, and the apparently self-deprecating use of the word "nigger." Yet, despite the genre's heavy emphasis on crime, violence, and abusive language, the *Times* was overwhelmingly positive toward gangsta rap throughout the period.[28]

In a 1989 feature article, "Rap as Public Forum on Matters of Life and Death," John Leland gave subtle praise to gangsta rap, "West Coast hip-hop has seized upon the persona of the gang members as a way to address Black-on-Black violence." The *Times* acknowledged gangsta rap as a public forum for African-American youth to articulate the harsh realities of life in America's inner cites. None of the gangsta rap articles in this period attributed any aspects of this harsh reality to possible structural flaws within the American social order. Instead, nearly all of the features on gangsta rap attributed pathologies prevalent among the American "underclass" solely to inadequacies among its own members. Moreover, gangsta rap as a genre was never subjected to the type of intense critical scrutiny previously leveled in the direction of radical rap.

The *Times* also acknowledged the emergence of female voices in hip-hop as an important thematic element. Though female personalities existed in each of the hip-hop genres previously mentioned, the *Times* coverage tended to segregate them into several features dealing with women in rap, irrespective of genre. Rather than present female performers as distinct artists in their own right, the *Times* features marginalized female rappers by emphasizing their reaction to the misogyny prevalent in male hip-hop.

Another consistent pattern placed African-American female rappers within a feminist model. In a July 1990 editorial by Michele Wallace, "When Black Feminism Faces the Music, and the Music Is Rap," the article featured a full-shot of Queen Latifah, but only peripherally covered the aesthetic or intellectual contributions of female rappers. Instead, most of the column space critiqued male-dominated hip-hop.[29]

By the 1990s, when the hip-hop phenomenon was a more broadly based cultural movement, the *Times* claimed hip-hop as a product of television: "How Rap Moves to Television's Beat." In this article, the longest on hip-hop to appear during the study period, the *Times* associated raps origins directly with commercial television.[30]

The 1990 controversy surrounding 2-Live Crew was the biggest hip-hop related story covered by the *Times*. The *Times* coverage of this controversial group and their subsequent obscenity trial only peripherally covered either 2-Live Crew or the dubious lyrical content of their music. The *Times* February spot news coverage, "Tape Obscenity Conviction Is Upset,"[31] indicated the *Times* response was overwhelmingly anti-censorship, and, as a result, more positive toward 2-Live Crew.

In 1990, just after a Fort Lauderdale judge ruled 2-Live Crew's album *As Nasty as They Wanna Be* obscene in the three Florida counties under his jurisdiction, there was a deluge of media coverage focusing on 2-Live Crew and hip-hop generally. In "Rap: Slick, Violent, Nasty and, Maybe Hopeful," *Times* critic Pareles defended hip-hop: "From its beginnings in the mid-1970s . . . rap has been met by condescension, rejection and outright fear from those outside its domain."[32]

As the legal case continued, the *Times* focused progressively less on 2-Live Crew and hip-hop and more on the broader issue of censorship. The newspaper gave coverage to the trials of both 2-Live Crew and the African-American record store owners who had been arrested for selling the group's censored album. The *Times* coverage of the 2-Live Crew trial was so intensive in October of 1990 that they printed an AP story about the jurors' request to laugh during the trial testimony because of physical pain experienced while restraining themselves.[33]

The *Times* coverage of the movement to censor unpopular expressions in hip-hop did not stop with 2-Live Crew. In August 1990, on the eve of the release of the first major-label album by the Geto Boys, the album was withdrawn by its distributor. The *Times* explained that Geffen Records "would not endorse its explicitly violent and sexual lyrics."[34] Furthermore, even though Pareles mentioned in passing that Geffen Records distributes controversial albums by white performers such as Andrew Dice Clay and the rock group Slayer, this double standard was never addressed.[35]

The public discourse surrounding hip-hop and the issue of censorship also was reflected in two letters to the editor appearing in the *Times* during 1990. Though the letters were written by authority figures, and therefore not necessarily representative of sentiments of the *Times* or its readership, they do note which viewpoints the editorial staff would elect to publish concerning rap music and the controversy surrounding it. Harvard professor Henry Louis Gates Jr.'s letter appeared during the height of the furor surrounding 2-Live Crew, only two days after he was quoted at length in a feature on hip-hop. A noted African-American scholar, Gates attempted to decode for white America the "objectionable" lyrics of 2-Live Crew within the context of African-American culture. He called for those who would censor creative expression to use the same criteria when judging hip-hop as they would for white rock and comedy acts. He also offered a few meticulously crafted words of warning (and perhaps accommodation) about expressions of bigotry in African-American "urban culture."[36] In the second letter, published after 2-Live Crew was acquitted on obscenity charges, Warner Communications executive Robert Morgado urged readers to heed the messages in hip-hop and confront reality "however it may offend or disturb."[37]

In 1990 alone Jon Pareles wrote eleven of the thirteen features appearing in the Pop View, Pop Life, and Critic's Notebook section of the *New York Times* "Arts" section. Moreover, his tone and his opinions varied relative to the genre or the personalities. Although Pareles had complained that the political content of Public Enemy's music had become "stubbornly, clumsily impolitic" when it became anti-Semitic, he defended 2-Live Crew and gangsta rappers, some of whom have become notorious for their verbal—even physical—attacks on black women. In the midst of the legal uproar over 2-Live Crew, Pareles became perhaps unwittingly self-reflexive, relative to his previous comments about Public Enemy, when he wrote about the "condescension, rejection and outright fear [of hip-hop] from those outside its domain."[38]

Although Pareles' articles were by far the most prominent of the nearly 20 staff and freelance journalists and critics used by the *Times* from 1985 to 1990, his viewpoints were on the whole relatively positive toward rap music, except for his features on Public Enemy. The *Times* staff music writers wrote the vast majority of the positive news items on hip-hop. When features appeared to be negative, they were usually written by the *Times* city or national staff, but only after the topical personality or genre had already been vilified in other media coverage. Hard news items, especially those that were negative, were usually obtained from freelance journalists or the wire services and represented a minority of the *Times* coverage.

The discursive practices which juxtaposed rap music with the iconography of social disorder at the *New York Times* had important implications on several levels. On perhaps the most obvious, the *Times*' important role as cultural gatekeeper and agenda setter for American elites meant that its performance vis-a-vis rap music simultaneously gave license to and structured the manner in which other mainstream media covered the genre. Much more work is needed on the precise nature of the dialogues within and among mainstream American media institutions seeking to make rap music intelligible to audiences and advertisers. On another level, the widespread circulation of discourses presenting the rap music/violence conflation as a formula for commercial success likely reached beyond the journalistic community to influence the attitudes, expectations and aesthetic choices of the music industry, rap performers and the culture overall.

On yet another level, any effort to understand the demonization of rap music in elite media discourses must take the historical moment into account. Within a context devoid of the Soviet threat, and in which direct invocations of race and class-based difference are to be assiduously avoided, news discourses seeking to comprehend rap music through the language of crime functioned metonymically to position African-American, working class youth as the Other against which the national identity is regulated and reaffirmed. This dimension of the *Times'* journalistic performance also tells an important story about how the emergence of the rap music/violence conflation helped to mediate longstanding anxieties related to race, class and generational difference.

In other ways too numerous to mention, the mainstream media's demonization of rap music in the period after the 2-Live Crew obscenity case set the stage for the ascendance of the Black urban gangsta as a marketable persona in the period to follow. But the role played by the *New York Times* in the rise—and now the demise—of gangsta rap is probably less important than the manner in which it clears space to think through how the globalization of markets and the need for new enemies in the post-Cold War era became manifest in the practices of elite journalism overall. A central feature of these practices was the shift from information to drama as the prevailing paradigm of mainstream news operations. Indeed not only was the dramatic model crucial to the *Times'* rap music journalism in the period 1985–1990, but it also helps to explain more recent 1990s scandal-driven cottage industries which have emerged around the O.J. Simpson trial, the death of Princess Diana, and current allegations of sexual misconduct and perjury by President Clinton. In each of these examples traditional boundaries separating information from entertainment, tabloid journalism from its more impartial, objective counterpart, have been erased. But while the *New York Times'* coverage of rap music dramatically illuminates the way the practice of mainstream journalism has been altered by the demise of Soviet communism, it illuminates just as clearly core features of the process whereby a uniquely American common sense(ibility) has remained intact.

NOTES

1. See John Leland, "Rap and Race," *Newsweek* 69 (June 29, 1992), 49. The term hip-hop used here refers not only to rap music, but to a larger cultural complex of urban youth culture incorporating language, dance, fashion, visual art, literature, and cinema. Though the centerpiece of this cultural formation has been rap music, the hip-hop formation also incorporates other distinct musical genres such as new jack swing, house music, and dance hall reggae.

2. Charles Henry, *Culture and African-American Politics* (Bloomington: Indiana University Press, 1990), 33.

3. The years 1985 to 1990 will be examined, when the *Times* first had any significant coverage of hip-hop, to when there was widespread acknowledgment of hip-hop as a pre-eminent form of popular culture and entertainment among American youth.

4. Luther Williams, "The Real Jazz Journalism: 'New York *Times*' Coverage of an American Art Form (1921–1929)," (University of Georgia, Department of Journalism, 1987), ERIC, ED 282251.

5. John Frohnmayer, *Out of Tune, Listening to the First Amendment* (Nashville: The Freedom Forum First Amendment Center, Vanderbilt University, 1994), 39.

6. Ibid.

7. Patrick Hill, "All Eyez on Them: Race, Rap Music Journalism, and the Manufacture of Deviance 1985-1992." (M.A. Thesis, University of Missouri, 1998). See the following sources also: Michael Rogin, *Ronald Reagan: The Movie and Other Episodes in Political Demonology* (Los Angeles: University of California Press, 1987), 236–240; Jimmie Reeves and Richard Campbell, *Cracked Cover Age: Television News, the Anti-Cocaine Crusade, and the Reagan Legacy* (Durham, NC: Duke University Press, 1994); Robert Entman, "Modern Racism and the Images of Black in Local Television News," *Critical Studies in Mass Communication* 7 (1990), 332–345; Jack Lule, "The Rape of Mike Tyson: Race, The Press and Symbolic Types." In Dan Berkowitz (Ed.), *The Social Meanings of News: A Text Reader* (Thousand Oaks, CA: Sage, 1997).

8. Tipper Gore, "Hate, Rape and Rap," *The Washington Post* (Letter to the Editor), 8 January 1990.

9. "'A Clockwork Orange' in Central Park," *U.S. News & World Report*, 8 May 1989, 10.

10. See for example, Howard Winant, "Amazing Race: Recent Writing on Racial Politics and Theory," *Socialist Review* 23:2 (1993), 161–183; "Postmodern Racial Politics in the United States: Differences and Inequality," *Socialist Review* 20:1 (Jan.-March 1990), 121–147.

11. Cornel West, *Race Matters* (Boston: Beacon Press, 1993), 5.

12. Stuart Hall, Chas Critcher, Tony Jefferson, John Clarke and Brian Roberts, *Policing the Crisis: Mugging the State, and Law and Order* (New York: Holmes & Meier, 1978).

13. James Carey, "A Cultural Approach to Communications," *Communication Research* 2 (1975), 1–22.

14. Bernard Berelson, *Content Analysis in Communication Research* (Glencoe, IL: Free Press, 1952); Richard W. Budd, *Content Analysis of Communications* (New York: Macmillan, 1967).

15. For quotes cited in this passage see the following sources: Ice-T, Robert Hilburn and Chuck Phillips, "For Gangsta' Style Rappers, Urban Explosion Is No Surprise," *The Los Angeles Times*, 2 May 1992, A7. Second quote in passage is taken from the cover of the conference brochure for "On the Beat: Rock 'n' Rap, Mass Media and Society, February 3–6, 1993, the University of Missouri-Columbia School of Journalism; re: Sister Souljah, David Mills, "Sister Souljah's Call to Arms: The Rapper Says the Riots Were Payback. Are You Paying Attention?," *Washington Post*, 13 May 1992, B1.

16. Williams, "The Real Jazz Journalism."

17. Ibid., 3.

18. Gaye Tuchman, "The Newspaper as a Social Movement's Resource." In *Hearth and Home: Images of Women in the Media*, ed. by Gaye Tuchman, Arlene Kaplan Daniels and James Benet (New York: Oxford University Press, 1978), 188–189.

19. Robert Palmer, "Rap Music Despite Adult Fire Broadens Its Teenage Base," *New York Times*, 21 September 1986, B23.

20. Robert Palmer, "Street-Smart Rapping Is Innovative Art Form," *New York Times*, 4 February 1985, C13.

21. Glenn Collins, "Rap Music, Brash and Swaggering, Enters Mainstream," *New York Times*, 29 August 1988, C15.

22. Peter Watrous, "Big Band Jazzmen and Rap Musicians: Soulmates," *New York Times*, 26 June 1988, 26.

23. Williams, "The Real Jazz Journalism," 7.

24. Although this is true for the period from 1985 to 1990, the media attention given to hip-hop and its personalities after the Los Angeles rebellions is far greater than at any previous period of the *Times*' coverage.

25. Jon Pareles, "Public Enemy, Loud and Angry, Is Far From Its Own Best Friend," *New York Times*, 26 December 1989, C15.

26. See the following *Times* articles on gangsta rap: John Leland, "Rap as Public Forum on Matters of Life and Death," 12 March 1989, Sec. II, p. 29; Peter Watrous, "Violence and Sexism," 19 September 1990, C18; and Jon Pareles, "Gangster Rap: Life and Music in the Combat Zone," 7 October 1990, 29.

27. Jon Pareles, "Radical Rap: Of Pride and Prejudice," *New York Times*, 16 December 1990, B1.

28. For a more extended and sophisticated discussion of gangsta rap, see Robin D. G. Kelley, "Kickin' Reality, Kickin' Ballistics: The Cultural Politics of Gangsta Rap in Postindustrial Los Angeles." In *Droppin' Science: Critical Essays on Hip Hop Culture and Politics*, ed. by William E. Perkins, (Philadelphia: Temple University Press, 1996).

29. Michele Wallace, "When Black Feminism Faces the Music, and the Music Is Rap," *New York Times*, 29 July 1990, B15.

30. Jon Pareles, "How Rap Moves to Television's Beat," *New York Times*, 14 January 1990, B1.

31. Peter Applebome, "Tape Obscenity Conviction Is Upset," *New York Times*, 23 February 1990, C19.

32. Jon Pareles, "Rap: Slick, Violent, Nasty and, Maybe, Hopeful," *New York Times*, 17 June 1990, D1.

33. "It's All Right to Laugh, Obscenity Jury Is Told," *New York Times*, 19 October 1990 (AP Wire Service).

34. Jon Pareles, "Distributor Withdraws Rap Album Over Lyrics," *New York Times*, 4 November 1990, E18.

35. Ibid., 18.

36. Henry Louis Gates, Jr., "2-Live Crew Decoded," *New York Times* (Letter to the Editor), 19 June 1990, E14.

37. Robert J. Morgado, "We Don't Have to Like Rap Music, But We Need to Listen," *New York Times* (Letter to the Editor), 4 November 1990, E18.

38. See all of the *Times*' articles by Jon Pareles cited elsewhere in these notes. However, the following are especially elucidating regarding his contradictory statements: "Radical Rap," 16 December 1990; "Gangster Rap," 7 October 1990; and "Rap: Slick, Violent," 17 June 1990.

Selected Bibliography

LEGAL CASES

Action for Children's Television v. FCC, 932 F.2d 1504 (D.C. Cir. 1991).

American Booksellers v. Webb, 919 F.2d 1493 (llth Cir. 1990).

Brandenberg v. Ohio, 395 U.S. 444 (1969).

Cinevision Corp. v. City of Burbank, 745 F. 2d 560, 567 (9th Cir. 1984), *cert. denied*, 471 U.S. 1054 (1985).

Citizens to Save WIFM v. Fed. Communications Committee, 506 F.2d 246, 251 Dis. C. 1974.

FCC v. Pacifica, 438 U.S. 726 (1978).

Ginsberg v. New York, 390 U.S. 629, 638 (1968).

Goodrich Broadcasting, Inc. v. FCC, 6 FCC Rcd. 2178 (1991).

In re Enforcement of Prohibitions Against Broadcast Indecency, 7 FCC Rcd 6464 (1992).

In re Evergreen Media Corp., 6 FCC Rcd 502 (1991).

In re Infinity Broadcasting Corp. of Pennsylvania, 3 FCC Rcd.

In re Liability of Nationwide Communications, Inc., 6 FCC Rcd 3695 (1990).

Jones v. Wilkinson, 800 F.2d 989 (1986); *aff'd* 480 U.S. 926 (1987).

Luke Records, Inc. v. Navarro, 960 F.2d 134 (1992).

Miller v. California, 413 U.S. 15 (1973).

New York v. Ferber, 458 U.S. 747 (1982).

Sable Communications v. FCC, 492 U.S. 115 (1989).

Schad v. Borough of Mount Ephraim, 452 U.S. 61 (1981).

Schenck v. U.S., 249 U.S. 47 (1919).

Southeastern Promotions, Ltd. v. City of Atlanta, 334 F. Supp. 634 (N.D., Ga. 1971).

United States v. Evergreen Media Corp., 832 F. Supp. 1183 (N.D. Ill. 1993).

Ward v. Rock Against Racism, 491 U.S. 781 (1989).

Yale Broadcasting Co. v. FCC, 478 F.2d. 594 (D.C. Cir.), *cert. denied*, 41 U.S. 914 (1973).

Young v. American Mini Theaters, 427 U.S. 50, *reh'g denied*, 429 U.S. 873 (1976).

BOOKS

Aquilla, Richard. *The Old Time Rock and Roll: A Chronicle of an Era 1954–1963*. New York: Schirmer Books, 1989.

Arnold, Matthew. *Culture and Anarchy*. New Haven, CT: Yale University Press, 1994.

Bayles, Martha. *Hole in Our Soul: The Loss of Beauty & Meaning in American Popular Music*. New York: The Free Press, 1994; rpt. Chicago: University of Chicago Press, 1996.

Bronson, Fred. *The Billboard Book of Number One Hits*. New York: Billboard Publications, 1985.

Curtis, James. *Rock Eras. Interpretations of Music and Society, 1954-1984*. Bowling Green, OH: Bowling Green State University Press, 1987.

DeCurtis, Anthony. *Present Tense Rock & Roll and Culture*. Durham, NC: Duke University Press, 1992.

Denisoff, R. Serge & Richard A. Person, eds. *The Sounds of Social Change: Studies in Popular Culture*. Chicago: Rand McNally, 1972.

Eisen, Jonathan. *The Age of Rock*. New York: Random House, 1969.

Falkenburg, Claudia & Andrew Solt, eds. *A Really Big Show. A Visual History of "The Ed Sullivan Show."* New York: Viking Studio Books, 1992.

Frith, Simon & Andrew Goodwin, eds. *On Record: Rock, Pop, and the Written Word*. New

York: Pantheon Books, 1990.

Frohnmayer, John. *Out of Tune, Listening to the First Amendment*. Nashville: The Freedom Forum First Amendment Center, Vanderbilt University, 1994.

Gilman, Sander. *Difference and Pathology: Stereotypes of Sexuality, Race and Madness*. Ithaca, NY: Cornell University Press, 1985.

Goldstein, Fred & Stan Goldstein. *Prime Time Television: A Pictorial History from Milton Berle to Icon Crest*. New York: Crown, 1983.

Gore, Tipper. *Raising PG Kids in an X-Rated Society*. Nashville: Abingdon Press, 1987.

Hall, Stuart, Charles Critcher, Tony Jefferson, John Clarke & Brian Roberts. *Policing the Crisis: Mugging the State, and Law and Order*. New York: Holmes & Meier, 1978.

Harris, Michael. *Always on Sunday. Ed Sullivan: An Inside View*. New York: Meredith Press, 1968.

Hebdige, Dick. *Subculture: The Meaning of Style*. London: Methuen & Co. Ltd., 1979.

Henry, Charles. *Culture and African-American Politics*. Bloomington: Indiana University Press, 1990.

Jones, Steve. *Rock Formation, Music, Technology, and Mass Communication, Foundations of Popular Culture*, vol. 3. Newbury Park, CA: Sage Publications, 1992.

Lipset, Seymour Martin & Earl Raab. *The Politics of Unreason: Right-Wing Extremism in America, 1790-1970*. New York: Harper & Row, 1970.

Lull, James. *Popular Music and Communication*, 2nd ed. Newbury Park, CA: Sage Publications, 1992.

Marsh, Dave. *Louie Louie*. New York: Hyperion, 1993.

Martin, Linda & Kerry Segrave. *Anti-Rock. The Opposition to Rock 'n' Roll*. Hamden, CT: Archon Books, 1988.

McCrohan, Donna. *Prime Time, Our Time. America's Life and Times Through the Prism of Television*. Rocklin, CA: Prima, 1990.

Newcomb, Horace. *Television: The Critical View*. New York: Oxford University Press, 1987.

Orme, Frank. *Television for the Family*. Los Angeles: National Association for Better Radio & Television, 1966.

Perkins, William E. *Dropping Science, Critical Essays on Hip Hop Culture and Politics*. Philadelphia: Temple University Press, 1996.

Reeves, Jimmie & Richard Campbell. *Cracked Coverage: Television News, the Anti-Cocaine*

Crusade and the Reagan Legacy. Durham, NC: Duke University Press, 1994.

Smith, Cecil. *Musical Comedy in America*. New York: Theatre Arts Books, 1950.

Stuessy, Joe. *Rock and Roll. Its History and Stylistic Development*. Englewood Cliffs, NJ: Prentice Hall, 1990.

Szatmary, David P. *Rockin' in Time. A Social History of Rock and Roll*. 2nd ed. Englewood Cliffs, NJ: Prentice Hall, 1991.

Tuchman, Gaye, Arlene Kaplan Daniels & James Benet, eds. *Hearth and Home: Images of Women in the Media*. New York: Oxford University Press, 1978.

Ward, Ed, Geoffrey Stokes, & Ken Tucker. *Rock of Ages. The Rolling Stone History of Rock & Roll*. New York: Summit Books, 1986.

West, Cornel. *Race Matters*. Boston: Beacon Press, 1993.

Wicke, Peter. *Rock Music. Culture, Aesthetics and Sociology*. Cambridge, MA: Cambridge University Press, 1987.

JOURNAL AND GENERAL ARTICLES

"ABC 'Blacklist' Stirs Folk People," *Billboard* (March 1963), 1,8.

Andrews, Edmund L. "The Media Business; Howard Stern Employer Faces $600,000 Fine," *New York Times*, Late Edition-Final 18 Dec. 1992, Al.

"Bar 'Protest' Songs from Europe GI's," *Variety* (August 1965), 1.

Berry, Cecile & David Wolin. "Comment, Regulating Rock Lyrics: A New Wave of Censorship?" *Harvard Journal on Legislation* 23:2 (Summer 1986), 606.

Bruck, Connie. "The Takedown of Tupac," *The New Yorker* (7 July 1997), 46-65.

Bundy, J. "Censored R & R on New MBS Disk Service Format," *Billboard* (August 1958), 2.

Campbell, Emily. "Obscenity, Music and the First Amendment: Was the 2-Live Crew Lively?" *Nova Law Review* 15:1 (Winter 1991), 159–240.

Casals, Pablo. "A Disgrace to Music," *Music Journal* XIX:1 (January 1961), 18.

"CBS (Ed Sullivan) Bans Folksinger Dylan for John Birch Satirization," *Variety* (May 1963), 2.

Entman, Robert. "Modern Racism and the Images of Black in Local Television News," *Critical Studies in Mass Communication* 7 (1990), 332-45.

"FCC Considers Fining Infinity," *Daily Variety* (30 November 1992), 16.

"FCC Daily Digest," Warren Publishing, Inc., *Communications Daily* (5 October 1989).

"FCC Fines Chicago Station $6,000 for Indecency," *Broadcasting* 117 (11 December 1989), 71.

"FCC Keeps New Fines Policy," *Television Digest 32* (25 May 1992), 4.

Flint, Joe. "Evergreen to Fight Indecency Charge: Since It Has No Avenue of Appeal for FCC Fine, It Will Refuse to Pay," *Broadcasting 122* (13 January 1992), 91.

Flood, Marilyn J. "Lyrics and the Law: Censorship of Rock-and-Roll in the United States and Great Britain," *New York Law School Journal of International and Comparative Law* 12:3 (Fall 1991), 402.

Fong-Torres, Ben. "Drugola Inquiry: Senator Claims Columbia Gag," *Rolling Stone* (16 August 1973), 8.

———. "Lennon Song: The Man Can't Fuck Our Music," *Rolling Stone* (February 1970), 1,6.

———. "When Humor Is No Longer Funny," *Rolling Stone* (July 1970), 8.

Gates, Henry Louis, Jr. "2-Live Crew Decoded," *New York Times* (Letter to the Editor), 19 June 1990, E14.

Goldberg, Michael. "At a Loss for Words: Record-Industry Acceptance of Stickering Is Already Having Chilling Effect," *Rolling Stone* (May 1990), 19–22.

———. "Crackdown on 'Obscene' Shows: New San Francisco Law Aimed at Rock 'n' Roll Concerts," *Rolling Stone* (30 January 1986), 9, 466.

Goldberg, Michael & Jeffrey Ressner. "Retailers Take on Stickering," *Rolling Stone* (April 1990), 26.

Gore, Tipper. "Hate, Rape and Rap," *Washington Post* (Letter to the Editor), 8 January 1990.

Greene, Michael. "Censorship May Be Just Around the Corner: Why Are These People Laughing?" *Billboard* (August 1986), 40.

Halonen, Doug. "Detroit FM Fined for 'Indecency,'" *Electronic Media* (9 October 1989), 42.

Holland, Bill. "Bush Ban on Indecent Radio Being Challenged," *Billboard* (12 September 1992), 82.

———. "Congressional (In)Action Good for Radio; Several Legislative Conflicts Go Broadcasters' Way," *Billboard* (15 October 1994), 96.

———. "FCC Delays Indecency Paper Again, Plans Winter Release," *Billboard* (3 December 1994), 100.

———. "NAB Gears Up to Fight Performance Right; Recording Industry Wants Copyright

Law Changed," *Billboard* (13 March 1993), 111.

―――. "Recession's Effects Resonated in Radio Rule-Making," *Billboard* (26 December 1992), "Radio" section, 83.

Kanzer, Adam M. "Misfit Power, the First Amendment and the Public Forum: Is There Room in America for the Grateful Dead?" *Columbia Journal of Law and Social Problems* 25:3 (1992), 521–65.

Krasnow, Erwin. "Government Regulation Persists; Media Audience Is the Victim," *Legal Times* (1 June 1987), 14.

Leland, John. "Rap and Race," *Newsweek* LXIX (29 June 1992), 49.

Light, Alan. "2-Live Crew Beats the Rap," *Rolling Stone* (November 1990), 27.

Love, Robert. "Washington Wives' Set Their Sights on Video," *Rolling Stone* (October 1985), 18.

McCormick, Jim. "Protecting Children from Music Lyrics: Sound Recordings and 'Harmful to Minors' Statutes," *Golden Gate University Law Review* 23:1-2 (Spring 1993), 689-92, 698-99.

McDonald, James R. "Censoring Rock Lyrics: A Historical Analysis of the Debate," *Youth and Society* 19:3 (March 1988), 296.

Mayer, Caroline E. "FCC Curbs Radio, TV Language; Agency Threatens Stations That Are Sexually Explicit," *Washington Post*, Final Edition, 17 April 1987, A1.

Moran, T. "Sounds of Sex," *New Republic* (12, 19 August 1985), 14-16.

Natter, Jeanine. "Un-Ban the Banned Band, A First Amendment Perspective on Banning Concerts," *Entertainment and Sports Lawyer* 9:2 (Summer 1991), 34, 36, 62, 72, 74.

Neely, Kim. "Louisiana Law to Require LP Stickers," *Rolling Stone* (August 1990), 35.

―――. "Rockers Sound Off," *Rolling Stone* (August 1990), 27-29.

Palmer, Robert. "Rap Music Despite Adult Fire Broadens Its Teenage Base," *New York Times*, 21 September 1986, B23.

Pareles, Jon. "Pop View; A Case Against Censoring Rock Lyrics," *New York Times*, Late City Final Edition, 3 May 1987, section 2, 22.

―――. "Public Enemy, Loud and Angry, Is Far From Its Own Best Friend," *New York Times*, 26 December 1989.

Sandow, G. " Doctors Deny PMRC Alliance," *Rolling Stone* (February 1990), 34.

Savage, David. "So Far, 'Shock Jock' Stern Has Had Last Word," *Los Angeles Times*, Home Edition, 15 December 1992, A5.

Seabrook, John. "The World of Television, Rocking in Shangri La," *The New Yorker* (10 October 1994), 64-78.

Seligman, Gerald. "Twelve States Consider 'Porn Rock' Legislation," *Rolling Stone* (June 1986), 19.

"Short Takes," *Daily Variety* (8 January 1993), 59.

Spiegelman, Arthur. "FCC Fines Howard Stern's Bosses $600,000 for Talking Dirty," *Reuters*, 18 December 1992, AM Cycle.

Stark, Phyllis. "FCC Ownership Caps, Indecency Fines Made Waves," *Billboard* (26 December 1992), Radio section, 80.

Sukow, Randy. "House Passes 6 A.M.- Midnight Indecency Ban; Communications Attorneys Say Provision Will Be Struck Down by Courts," *Broadcasting* 28 (10 August 1992), 122.

Talerman, Jason. "The Death of Tupac: Will Gangsta Rap Kill the First Amendment?" *Boston College Third World Law Journal* 14:1 (Winter 1994), 138.

Vatz, Edward J. "You Can't Play That, A Selective Chronology of Banned Music: 1850–1991," *School Library Journal* 37 (July 1991), 7.

Wharton, Dennis. "Infinity Hit with 600G Stern Fine," *Daily Variety* (21 December 1992), 3.

Winant, Howard. "Amazing Race: Recent Writing on Racial Politics and Theory," *Socialist Review* (1993), 23, 161–83.

———. "Postmodern Racial Politics in the United States: Differences and Inequality," *Socialist Review* 20 (January/March 1990), 121–47.

"Yeh-Heh-Heh-Hes, Baby," *Time* LXVII:25 (18 June 1956), 54.

Zoglin, Richard. "Shock Jock; Howard Stern Is Shaking up Radio—and the FCC—With His Raunchy, Racist, In-Your-Face Talk, but Listeners Seem to Love It," *Time* (30 November 1992), 72.

Zucchino, David. "Big Brother Meets Twisted Sister," *Rolling Stone* (November 1985), 9.

Index

About the Editors and Contributors

MICHAEL J. BUDDS, associate professor, is the coordinator of music history and literature at the University of Missouri-Columbia. He is the author of *Jazz in the Sixties* (2nd ed., 1990), the co-author of *Rock Recall* (1993), a contributor to *Women & Music: A History* (1991), and the editor of *Monographs and Bibliographies in American Music*.

SANDRA DAVIDSON, associate professor of journalism and adjunct associate professor of law at the University of Missouri-Columbia, has written legal studies in *William and Mary Bill of Rights Journal*, *Hastings Communication and Entertainment Law Journal*, and *Law-Technology*.

LINDSEY R. FORE has researched rock music in the American press as part of her Master's graduate work at Southern Illinois University.

PATRICK B. HILL, a doctoral candidate in the American Culture program at the University of Michigan, Ann Arbor, is completing a study of elite journalism's coverage of rap music and African-American youth culture since the end of the Cold War. His other degrees are from Washington University, St. Louis, and the University of Missouri-Columbia.

DAVID SLAYDEN, an associate professor in the School of Journalism and Mass Communication at the University of Colorado-Boulder, is the author of studies on hate speech and the demise of discourse in the computer age. He once was a drummer in a rock band.

JEFFREY L. L. STEIN is the McElroy Chair in Communication Arts and Executive-in-Residence at Wartburg College in Waverly, Iowa. A graduate of the University of Iowa College of Law, he is also executive secretary of the Iowa Broadcast News Association.

STEPHEN H. WHEELER, an associate professor of history at Northeast State Technical Community College (Blountville, Tenn.), is currently examining the relationship between television military sitcoms and the Vietnam War. His degrees are from the University of Mississippi.

BETTY HOUCHIN WINFIELD, professor of journalism and adjunct professor of political science at the University of Missouri-Columbia, has published studies on political communication, including Hillary Clinton's image (1997), *Two Commanders-in-Chief: Free Expression's Most Severe Test* (1992), and *FDR and the News Media* (1994, 1990).

ISBN 0-313-30705-9

90000>

EAN

9 780313 307058

HARDCOVER BAR CODE